TRAVELING SUNWISE

JACQUELINE MARTIN

For Meghan
Embrace your beautiful heart

"Life is a pure flame, and we live by an invisible Sun within us."

–*Sir Thomas Browne*

INTRODUCTION

This book is about diving for pearls; going deep to find the dirt encrusted gems of our lives that make us who we are and then relaxing into ourselves.

When I was initially diagnosed with cancer, I had the naïve notion that I had inadvertently taken a wrong turn in my life and if I could identify that wrong turn and right it, then my temporarily derailed life would be back on track. I tricked myself into believing it would be that simple and I began the process of traveling back in time through my life, stopping at every crossroad to have a look around. I began digging and the more I dug the more gems I found. Many were wrapped in horrific packages, like rape and abuse, but those were ultimately the most precious gems of all.

Some events in our lives drag us to our knees and it is there that we hear the voice of God. Then we feel divine strength seeping into the cracks and crevices of our lives and we know we are changed.

I have come to believe that my story is a small entry into our collective story; that my suffering is your suffering and it is sacred. We don't have to become our misery; we can give it back to the source. It is our choice: we can live broken or we can reclaim our beautiful life and soar.

This book is a story about choosing your one true, authentic life and letting the other ones go; the ones that no longer fit and probably never did. It is about healing and becoming whole. And it is about how the Divine works in our lives as we claw our way back to life.

PROLOGUE

Our day was brilliant and here in New England, we relish days such as this: warm rich summer sun, gentle breeze, sapphire blue sky, exquisite long views of our rolling hills and absolutely no humidity. It is a reminder of why we live here and why we withstand the long, dark, difficult winters. I imagined it was my gift because on this day, fifty years earlier, I was born in London, England, the third of five children. I like to think that day too, was warm and welcoming.

Many of my friends found turning fifty tumultuous, but for me it felt good - no heavy looming decisions about school, marriage, child bearing, child rearing, career paths, or geographical destination. My life was affirming: the children were both off to college; my husband and I had found a good, comfortable rhythm, our careers were on track and I no longer felt the need to prove myself like I did in my younger years.

Some birthdays seem more demanding of decisions that we aren't always prepared to make, like turning thirty. That was a traumatic birthday for me because I felt an overwhelming pressure to make the decision of whether or not to have children before my peak fertility years were history. I didn't want to think about that ticking biological clock in my early thirties. Turning fifty wasn't like that. My two dear friends were taking me to lunch to welcome me into the club – the over fifty club – which they feel is one of the greatest honors and joys in life. Their reasoning is that, at the mid-point of our lives, supposedly the more difficult years are behind us and we have earned the title of "wise women." The years to come, they determined, would be softer and easier. That sounded good to me so I was happy to join the club. We were having lunch on the terrace of the Hopkins Inn overlooking the indigo waters of Lake Waramaug and the perfect weather matched the festive occasion. I told my friends, Eileen and Cindy, that I would order a warm, gorgeous day to mark this auspicious turning, and I did.

I'm often teased about having a direct line to the Heavens; that my calls are always answered. I smiled as I thought about this, knowing it was all a matter of perspective. I think we all have a direct line – it's about choosing to use it. While I was happily anticipating the warmth of the sun, great friends and delicious food, I was also preoccupied with the results of a biopsy that I was to receive later that afternoon. But, there was no point in letting that ruin the day and I didn't. I had a spectacular fiftieth birthday lunch, complete with decadent desserts, gifts and giggles.

When I returned home, I made that call to my friend to get the results of the breast biopsy. His hesitation spoke volumes and I found myself comforting him and telling him it wasn't so bad, that it was an excellent opportunity for growth, and that my portfolio of life had been missing some good old fashion diseases, so this would round it out. But that was false bravado because I knew that invasive lobular carcinoma is no laughing matter. When I hung up the phone, I relinquished my grip on cheerfulness and stood motionless, in total devastation and disbelief. I felt that I was straddling two worlds and I needed a moment to collect myself so that I could catch up with my life before that phone call. I had vague memories of having these feelings in my past, when I felt blind-sided and all the blood left in my body started beating like a drum in my head, blocking out everything else that was familiar; I just couldn't recall when or what would have caused me to feel this way. I didn't move a muscle, my mind floated from numbness to disbelief, denial, devastation, and deep sadness. I don't know how long I stood there like that but it seemed like hours.

The human psyche is brilliantly resilient; it has an incredible ability to go into denial in order to protect us. Thankfully, this kicked in very quickly and I told myself that my results must have been mixed up with someone else's, that it was all a big mistake, that I would call my friend, an oncologist, and he would get it all straightened out with the radiology department, that it would just take a few phone calls and my temporarily derailed life would be back on track. And so I began to breathe again and the roaring in my ears stopped and I took a step toward the chair and sat down. But I knew I had a problem. I have been blessed, or cursed, with this deep knowing about certain things in life (particularly my body). I was the one who actually called in the biopsy because for two years I had been encouraging my gynecologist to pay attention to this growing tumor in my left breast. She claimed it was not pathological based on two previous mammograms. I wasn't buying that so I decided to advocate for myself, which put me in an uncomfortable situation where I was not only the referring physician but also the patient receiving the wrenching diagnosis. That is why I chose to stay in limbo, between truth and denial, until I could collect myself and figure out a plan. I decided to fix a cup of tea – this was very familiar ground, something I have been doing for close to forty years. Yet this day, I had to think about what I was doing. This familiar ritual kept me engaged and in the moment. Finally, I sat down with my steaming cup of tea and waited for my husband to come home. Speaking about this with him would bring me back from the precipice; the scales would tip away from denial and towards reality and that could wait.

The hot tea began to soothe and comfort me and I let my mind wander but not too close to the "C" word: What would I do? Allopathic medicine wasn't my thing and neither were hospitals; I birthed both my children at home to avoid hospitals; the only thing worse than cancer, was the treatment; I hadn't seen great results with natural approaches to cancer and yet I'd heard of a few people who ate a macrobiotic diet and lived to tell the story. My mind continued to spin out of control - perhaps the tumor just felt big but was actually small enough that I could still qualify for a lumpectomy; and on and on until I closed my eyes and asked God to take over. Yet, deep in my soul I had the feeling that somewhere on this journey called "Life" I had taken a wrong turn, a turn in a direction that didn't authenticate who I am; a turn where breathing became labored and my heart stopped singing; a turn towards uneasiness, discontent and illness; a turn towards cancer.

Later, when John arrived home, we spoke about this diagnosis very calmly and objectively as though we were speaking about an acquaintance. We placed our emotions on a very high shelf where they could remain safe and distant, not threatening. This worked temporarily while we collected and researched information about my particular breast cancer. Yet, we both knew without discussion that we would ultimately have to deal intimately with this illness.

PART ONE

"Looking Back"

CHAPTER ONE

The Search

Whom shall I call upon, If not him
who is dark and more of night than night itself.
The only one who wakes without a light
yet has no fear; the deep one, as yet
unspoiled by the light, the one of whom I know
because in trees he bursts forth from the earth
and because as fragrance
he rises softly from the soil
into my down bent face.

—Rilke

Invasive Lobular Carcinoma – sure doesn't have a nice ring to it. I pictured a little army of bad cells with spears, lined up, row after row, ready to invade at the commander's directive. They had little armor suits with face shields, much like in the times of King Arthur. They were short and round and full of anger and venom and I was wondering who let them into my body. All this was floating around my brain as I typed those words on my computer – Invasive lobular carcinoma, Aggressive lobular carcinoma, Infiltrating lobular carcinoma, it was all the same thing and not the best cancer to have; not that any of them are easy. I had no knowledge about these things at that time so I called my friend Jedd, knowing that to discuss it with him would make it real. I'll never forget what he said when I asked him if he would be willing to be my oncologist even though we were friends. He said he would be honored to treat me. Soon, I would be honored to be his patient.

Weeks went by, second and third opinions were offered, all the questions were answered about size, margins, grade, etc. and a protocol was determined. I have leaned towards a healthy, natural lifestyle since my early college years. I ate healthfully; exercised regularly; supplemented my diet with nutrients; and aligned myself with natural and complementary health care whenever I was experiencing a physical, emotional or spiritual imbalance. Given this early natural approach to health, it is no surprise that I became a chiropractic Physician and acupuncturist. This allowed me to serve others who chose to heal in a way that supported the body's natural ability to right itself. I am absolutely in love with the miracle of the body and its innate intelligence; I am in awe of its ability to make a correction, given some assistance, and to remove blockages and open pathways that have shut down in response to trauma. It has been an honor to have practiced this way and "to do no harm." Given my strong beliefs about health and healing, it may seem contradictory that I never considered exclusively alternative cancer treatments. I was scared to death because I had watched so many friends and acquaintances bravely succumb to cancer. I didn't want to die and, while the thought of allopathic or traditional cancer treatment was repulsive to me, I had observed in my twenty-five years of practice that most of my patients and friends who chose traditional treatment over alternative treatment had fared slightly better. However, those who took a broad view that included both an allopathic and a complementary approach, fared the best.

I decided I would have the surgery. It seemed logical to remove the mass. I wanted to have a few rounds of chemo first to try to shrink the tumor so that a lumpectomy would be possible. That, however, was not to be. I would complete the rest of the chemo following surgery. I negotiated the number of chemo treatments to roughly 70% of what was suggested because I knew that was all my body could take. It was heart breaking for me to come to terms with what I believed about health and healing and what I had chosen to do to my body. I struggled to reconcile these feelings as both a patient and a doctor but I couldn't. Ultimately, I think that fear guided me in a direction I wouldn't typically have chosen.

We make decisions based upon many things, not the least of which is how our choices will affect the people we love most. My son had just started his first year of college in California and would not have to witness my illness day to day the way my daughter would. He is sweet and sensitive and is comfortable with his emotions. My daughter's sensitivity is like an exquisite mountain lake: deep and inviting but difficult to get to because of the steep rugged terrain that surrounds and protects it. However, once you are in, it is like coming home. Her love is a cozy comforter warming my soul. I could not bear to imagine either of these precious beings motherless when they were just beginning to get their feet under them. Meghan had just begun her senior year in high school. This was her year to shine; no older brother around to overshadow her wonderful accomplishments or to share her parents' love and attention. And then there was my husband. He thinks I'm invincible and saw my cancer as a temporary setback. So, as a mother and wife, I made decisions about my treatment that would be best for the entire family. Deep in my soul, I knew better than to poison my body with drugs in the hope that wellness was on the other side of that. And I also knew that the extensive, barbaric, tram flap surgery to remove a half dollar size tumor was overkill. I chose the tram flap surgery anyway for two reasons: I did not want unnatural substances like saline or silicon in my body, and secondly, I did not want to wake up without a breast because that would be too demoralizing and would affect my recovery. I chose the tram flap treatment so that it would be over quickly, I could begin to get well, and life would be back to normal - our family would be back to normal.

I did not expect the horrors of chemotherapy: I did not expect every bodily system to be negatively affected by these drugs. I did expect to be tired, which I was. Yet, I still   continued to work because it made me feel normal and kept my spirits high. I did not expect to be so bothered by being bald because my father always said I had a beautiful head! Isn't it great how we grab onto what suits us at the time? I remember my mother telling me she loved me and how incredibly beautiful I was. I chose to believe that, too, until that fateful day when I was thirty-seven and plucking my eyebrows for the first time. There I was, face pressed against the mirror, tweezers in hand, and I realized that I was not at all beautiful. I started laughing uncontrollably, holding immense gratitude for my mother and that wonderful lie she had told me repeatedly through much of my life; it simply took beauty, as an issue, off the table. Until that day, I assumed I was beautiful and I felt beautiful and that is really all that matters: how we feel about ourselves. I never wondered if I was pretty during those awkward teenage years, because I knew I was – my mom said so!

I was wrong to think that being bald wouldn't be an issue. When people say, "Bald is beautiful," I believe it applies largely to men; women simply look better with hair! I was also wrong to think I wasn't vain; I was! Some mornings, feeling less than cheery, I would look in the mirror at those bright red scars all over my body and not a lick of hair anywhere and I would weep from the depths of my soul and ask, "What has happened to you, Jacqui?" But then I would pray for courage and hope, get dressed, and go to work. I didn't want to hang out in that pity place too long for fear it would envelope me.

When I see suffering in the face of others, I am unable to simply witness their pain; I want to fix or dampen it.

I have to remind myself that perhaps this is also their journey and not exclusively mine. It was heartbreaking for me to look into the eyes of   loved ones and see their sadness and anger for what they perceived as the injustice of my cancer. I didn't share those feelings, yet, for their benefit, I exhibited a false bravado that sometimes seeped into me in a gloriously positive way and other times threatened to suffocate me. That is why, on those mornings when I couldn't carry the burden of sadness, suffering, pain and betrayal for myself and everyone else, I would wait until my husband had gone to work and my daughter to school and I would dismiss the "cheerleader" part of me and cry all those burning tears that everyone was holding back. It was like I had released the dam that was holding my tears and when all the tears were spilled, my body relaxed and I felt calmness come over me.

Work was my refuge then, as it always has been, because it takes me completely away from myself and allows me to focus on others. I feel grounded when I work with patients and for this I am both humbled and grateful. Stepping away from sadness and despair towards gratitude and power drove me forward and lightened my heart.

And so the medical journey began. But there was another journey developing inwardly. I began wondering if there was a time in my life when I had inadvertently chosen the wrong turn - the turn that had put me on the path towards cancer. There was no history of cancer in our family. My diet is healthy; I'm not an excessive drinker or into drugs, and my life seemed to me to be mostly in balance. So, it had to be something deeper than the physical. I believe most physical illness starts many years earlier as an energetic disconnect in the mind/ body/spirit, so I began there – looking for a disconnect. I had this persistent feeling that my cancer was a wake up call but I didn't know what that meant. I did know that this was a rich opportunity to uncover that point in my life where I had turned down the road of discontent and emotions began to fester and create chaos in my body. I believed my life depended on uncovering this mystery.

Over the years, I hypothesized that healing was related to attitude, faith, hope and the dominant archetypical patterns governing each individual.

We each have archetypical patterns that define our behavior and how we make our way in the world, like artist, Olympian or wizard. We also share the more common or dominant archetypes like child and victim. I love the world of archetypes, not just in theory but also in practice. I remember the classic archetypes in the Fairy Tales from my childhood: Snow White, Sleeping Beauty and of course, Cinderella. Who doesn't dream about becoming rags to riches princess like Julia Roberts in *Pretty Woman?* The discussion of Archetypes can be traced back as far as Plato but we are probably more familiar with these prototypical behaviors from Greek Mythology: Aphrodite, goddess of love, Zeus, and my favorite, Athena, the warrior of wisdom, love, and the arts. Shakespeare's work is also full of archetypical characters. Perhaps *Romeo and Juliet* is the most well known because of the beautiful story itself, but also because of all the numerous copycats; we find them in songs, shows, and movies, and they are based on this classic story of forbidden love, heartbreak and ultimately loss. One of my favorite renditions of this archetypical love story is *West Side Story* and, far more recently *Broke Back Mountain*. But it was the Swiss psychologist Carl Jung who brought the study of archetypes to the forefront in his use of archetypes as a means of therapy; an explanation for why certain behaviors existed and how they could help the patient with self-discovery and ultimately, relationships. Today, many people in the field of Complementary Medicine also utilize archetypes and their implications as a therapeutic tool.

Both the "victim" and the "martyr" archetypes kept creeping into my consciousness as I began investigating personality types and cancer. I have been a victim many times in my life but I never imagined that I had embraced this as a way of walking through life. I've tried to learn from this archetype not to be a victim but to come from a position of strength and courage. This is the beauty of archetypes: they are rich with potent lessons. They teach us how we want to be and allow us to gather the strength we need to move around the darker side of that. For example the prostitute: she teaches us that we don't have to sell our soul for what we want, we can use our intelligence to figure out a better way.

The single most revealing characteristic of the victim for me was that she doesn't claim the happiness that she deserves and that sounded a lot like me. For the martyr, it was that she has suffered and held onto that suffering for far too long. It is this single glaring quality that tells me that the martyr is a strong presence in my life. This understanding has helped me make some tremendous changes in my behavior that will hopefully lead to a more healthy life.

Archetypes, in and of themselves, are neither good nor bad, they simply are. They teach us how to have a better relationship with ourselves and others by identifying patterns of behavior that we exhibit and that keep us out of balance, unhappy and separated from our best self. When I mentioned to a friend that I thought I was a martyr, she said, "yes, and who do you think is on the other end of that continuum?" I had to pause and think about that one for a moment, and then I realized I am a classic example of martyr/tyrant. A possible lesson for me is to not beat myself down; to step out of the way and allow myself freedom to grow with no resentment, no judgment, no suffering and no blame. In that respect, the Martyr archetype has been a marvelous teacher.

It is possible that cancer has nothing at all to do with hopelessness, an unwillingness or inability to forgive, victim or martyr archetype, anger or resentment, karma or genes. Perhaps it is a test, or an opportunity. Maybe it was simply a gift wrapped in the most awful of packages. I didn't know but I felt an urgency to explore this idea of taking the wrong turn because, given that feeling, I also realized that to get well, I would need to know what this wrong turn was; what it looked like, how it felt, how it shaped who I became, why it had such an impact on my life and, most importantly, whether I was willing to change. This became my preoccupation those first few months following my diagnosis.

CHAPTER TWO

The Eyes Have it

"Let whoever seeks not cease from his seeking until he finds.
When he finds he will be troubled. When he is troubled,
he will marvel and reign over all."

*Statement made by Jesus according to the
Gospel of St. Thomas found in Eygypt in 1945.*

I have always been a seeker. I don't know if there is a "seeker" gene on those beautifully beaded DNA strands but I know that it cannot be ignored. I have tried. I have told myself that there will be no more digging and searching, that it is time to take life at face value; that life is just as it seems. My earliest memory of being a seeker and being in love with the Divine was in second grade. I loved the ceremony of Mass. I was Catholic then and I loved the beautiful sound of the organ and the sweet voices of the choir. I loved the smell of incense and how it seeped into my soul and I loved its smoky aftermath. I loved the mysterious chanting in Latin. But mostly, I loved the sacraments. At age seven, I fantasized that one day bad guys would come into the church – Non-Catholics – and I would be the one to save the host. When everyone was busy fighting and screaming, I would march my three-foot tall body up to the altar, climb up the sacristy, gather the hosts together, eat them, and thus save the body and blood of Christ. What child thinks like this? It was pure lunacy and yet that was my preoccupation each time I sat in those shiny, smooth, hand carved brown wooden pews that lined up, row after row, facing the front of the church. I believed I would be a modern day Joan of Arc. I am happy to report that I no longer have this fantasy. I have, however, continued to seek. Often, I am on this journey alone but sometimes I bring other people into my search like therapists, healers, Shamans, Gurus, Saints, guides and of course the Divine; She is always present.

One of those therapists told me that our entire story, absolutely everything, was in the eyes. She asked me to bring in all my baby pictures. Then she covered my entire face, leaving only the eyes peering back. This, she claimed, would reveal the entire truth. So, I started with the pictures. I dug them all out: volumes of photos from childhood, adolescence, young adulthood, wedding, pregnancies, births, children's birthdays, graduations, first office, second office, first home, second, third and fourth homes, family of origin, family of procreation - all of them. As I looked at myself in each picture, I covered the rest of my face with my thumbs. Then I looked deeply into my eyes, looking to see if they would, as she had said, reveal everything.

Now, twenty-five years later, I don't remember what we discovered about those baby pictures. I do know now where she was going with this subtle but powerful investigation into my childhood. She was looking for abuse or a disconnection that can often be seen in the vacant eyes of children caught in photos. Unfortunately, we have all seen this in the eyes of neglected children and even in the eyes of adults.

I was unwilling to go there with her at that time in my life, my early thirty's; I was unwilling to even entertain the possibility of wrongdoing, so I didn't. The eyes are the windows of the soul and if you look deeply, you can see hurt, sadness, anger, fear and most definitely love, bliss and joy. I have continued to look deeply into others' eyes when I want to know more about them. But as I looked deeply into my own eyes in all those pictures, nothing significant to my exploration emerged.

I was taken by my mother's beauty in the family photos. Each new picture showed her with yet another child. She made motherhood look easy but I know there were many challenging times for her, especially as we got older and we acted on our strong beliefs of how life should unfold.

We were seven: Mom and Dad and the five of us children. Many years ago, a therapist described my family as "interesting." By the look on her face, I understood her to also mean amusing, alarming, befuddling and off-putting. I believed my family was a cohesive group of seven people who cared deeply about one another and there was nothing abnormal about that. I have noticed this about families – people looking in are often aghast because it is not their reality. Families are like that and while we might not choose them, we love them just the same.

My father fell in love with my mother in 1947 on a crowded trolley car on the streets of Philadelphia. They were both rushing to get to work. He was a strapping, young, arrogant University of Pennsylvania graduate student. My mother was a gorgeous, svelte brunette with great joi de vivre and was a nursing student at Philadelphia General. He spotted this exquisite looking woman pushing her way onto the train and he said, "That is the woman I am going to marry." And he did. No two people could be more different and yet they were devoted to one another and were married for fifty-seven years when my mother passed away.

My father is a mystery to me. Perhaps his long career with the CIA trained him to keep things close to the vest. When all of us kids were home for holidays, we would jokingly commit to getting Dad drunk so that we could find out what really happened to JFK. It never worked, of course (neither the getting drunk nor learning what really happened to our forty- third president), and his answer always remained the same, "You kids read the newspapers just like me."

Dad expected a lot from himself and from us and I think he was disappointed on both fronts. I know that for the greater part of my life, I never felt good enough in his eyes. Now, as I write, I am wondering when all that changed and, more importantly, when I stopped caring.

It must have been sometime in my mid-forties when he fell off the pedestal and I started pleasing me instead of him. Of course, he never asked to be up there wobbling on that precarious pedestal. I willingly placed him there as children do.

I know little about my father's upbringing but know it is difficult to give what you didn't get. His parents weren't soft and cuddly and neither was he but he loved us deeply and wished only for our happiness, success and safety. He also insisted that we be well educated. This was his way of showing love. Beyond that, he deferred to my mother with regard to parenting.

Age has softened my father, as has my mother's passing. He is far more willing to engage with his children one to one since my mother is no longer present to be the buffer.

My mother was a strong, determined, clever woman who loved her children fiercely. It would be painfully unwise to stand between her and her children (as many nuns can attest to). She was unable to be objective about us and it took years before she could acknowledge that any of us were flawed.

Mom worked as a nurse in the early years of her marriage. She had a lot of energy and many friends. She also had the five of us, which kept her busy.

I don't think life turned out exactly the way my mother hoped it would; she would have preferred more glamour and more fun. She seemed to create that for herself until her fifties when my father retired. After retirement, he withdrew from their busy social life which was largely connected to his job with the C.I.A. My mother, who was naturally a more social being than my father, then reached out to her girlfriends. She filled her days with antiquing and wandering around the area looking for good deals on furniture that she could then re-finish and transform into beautiful pieces to sell for a tremendous profit. This filled her days but that exuberant piece of her that required constant acknowledgement for both her beauty and her charm, seemed to die and nothing replaced it; so she became less vibrant. Her legacy was her beautiful heart for which I am eternally grateful.

Carolyn is the oldest child. She was born when my parents were still living with my father's mother and his brother in a brownstone on the south side of Philly. She would say she is an anarchist but I would say that she has struggled to find her way. She loved law school but never liked practicing law so she has spent her time trying to find something that will excite her. We are often at odds in our thinking but I love her, her kindness and her complete lack of judgment.

Dick was born in Philadelphia eighteen months after Carolyn. He was kind and sweet and naturally the brightest and most talented of all the children. In his late teens, he was diagnosed as paranoid schizophrenic, which completely changed the direction of his life. The medication for this illness deadens the part of the brain that is delusional, and in the process obliterates the creative and emotional part. However, it keeps the patient functional which is critical. When Dick stays on his medicine, he is capable and responsible and even now, he will bring us all to task if he feels we are pulling too far away from the family. We are all grateful for that.

I was born 18 months following my brother in London in 1951. Based on studies of birth order, I would say I am a classic representative of the middle child. Early on I was painfully shy, introverted, terribly sensitive, a people pleaser and seemingly easy going. Today, I'm not so shy but I have a natural tendency towards introversion. I am a seeker, I am driven and I am determined to find my place in the world. Life has opened me up and softened my edges.

Judy is the fourth born. As a child, she was teeny tiny, timid, shy and even more sensitive than I was. Towards the end of high school and into college she was wild, earthy and a free spirit. She has a marvelous sense of humor and joi de vivre and we were great pals through college and early adulthood. I think that over the years, disappointment and disillusionment have whittled away at her soft heart and vitality.

Danny is the youngest. He is five years younger than I am and growing up, those five years seemed unbridgeable. In my thirties the discrepancy dissolved and we became great pals. Like my mother's beautiful heart, he is generous and kind and sees life and people through rose tinted glasses. He is a giver and has no expectations of anyone but himself.

This is a brief description of my family. I grew up with their love, support and protection and they shaped and re-shaped who I am.

I reach for the rest of the pictures and keep searching.

There I was in the old blue jeep in Saipan; the one in which mom had first learned to drive; there I was giggling as a youngster at the Oktoberfest in Germany.

Because of my father's career, we lived all over the world, moving every two to four years. I looked at all the different school pictures - five different high schools, and four different universities. Jumping around like that was difficult because I was never able to lay down roots; to have continuity with studies or with people, or to forge lasting friendships during those tender, awkward years. I believe this has made it difficult for me to establish long lasting relationships. I also have found that I tend to "move on" to new people, places, studies and activities. I do this when complacency sets in or when there is a lull in my life that makes me feel as though I am not accomplishing enough.

I resume my eye search through the wonderful pictures showing my two-year backpacking expedition through Great Britain, Europe and Africa between the end of graduate school and the beginning of my chiropractic studies. I smile at the pictures of my early romance and subsequent marriage and the blossoming of a new family. My second child was over 10 pounds and I was huge. The picture looked like a very large and colorful beach ball sitting on two sticks with a head on top. I can't imagine what I was thinking when I bought that maternity top.

I poured over those pictures for hours looking for a clue, some sign that I was heading for trouble. I looked deeply into those eyes, the defiant chin, a missing smile, a vacant look, or a postural change that screamed "cancer," and I found nothing. But I persisted; I was driven to discover where I veered off track and how it ultimately leads to illness.

Various spiritual traditions suggest that we contract for a particular life prior to incarnating; we grow more conscious through our experiences with betrayal, pain, love, joy, illness, recovery, heartbreak, dying and resurrecting. The hard part is not the challenges, no matter how severe, but how we internalize the lessons and learn from these challenges; and what we become and how we unfold as a result of these lessons. Starting at a very young age, every hurtful experience, no matter how small or large, chisels away at our innocence and trust, and thus our pure hearts. Likewise, every sweet, splendid experience opens our hearts to love and all the inherent possibilities that love offers. I suspect I got hung up here, in the realm of emotions. Perhaps, I thought I'd handled emotional challenges well, but the powerful emotions accompanying some of these ordeals were buried deep inside, invisible, crippling my capacity to experience joy and happiness. I was looking for these particular life experiences with an open mind and heart and I realized that those pictures could not help me. So I changed it up, took a deep breath and asked myself, "What is my first memory of not being okay, feeling sad, fearful, or disconnected?" This process was like looking through a Rolodex in which every incident in your life has been chronologically filed and at the bottom of each card is the dominant emotion each experience elicited. Searching for my first major emotional disconnection, I realized it was when I was four years old and living in Saipan.

Saipan is a tropical island located between the northern Pacific Ocean and the Philippine Sea. The closest country to the north is Japan and to the south is New Guinea. In 1944, the United States forced the Japanese out, and claimed it as a United States territory. Over the years, Saipan has become a beautiful resort, but in 1954 it was still remote and sparse. The CIA transferred my father to Saipan because of the political climate in Japan and because, after Pearl Harbor, Saipan was a supply and staging area for the U.S. Military. I remember my fourth Christmas in Saipan. It was very hot and humid - no snow or snowmen, no sledding or ice skating after school like in Germany; no winter coats or warm winter boots; no rushing home for hot chocolate and cookies after hours playing outside with friends. Instead, I remember Santa arriving, via helicopter, to the island. Everyone would run out of their houses to meet Santa when he landed. Children would yell with glee because Santa had a huge bag of presents. But I wasn't there; I was still in the house looking for my black patent leather shoes. I was wearing a brand new taffeta dress; the skirt was green and white checked and the top was solid green with a white collar. It felt a little scratchy around the waist but it looked beautiful, especially when I twirled around and the skirt flew straight out like a ballerina. My mother made all our clothes, so my older sister was wearing the exact same dress but with black and white checks and my younger sister's was blue with blue and white checks. One of our family jokes was that my youngest sister Judy, had to wear the same dress, in different colors, for a good ten years of her life as it was handed down from sister to sister! This was particularly annoying if she hated the dress to begin with (which she often did).

I searched for my shoes while all of my siblings were already outside. My older sister had to be on the square early because she was Mrs. Santa Clause in the Christmas pageant. As I scrambled around, my mother screamed for me to hurry up and find my shoes because Santa was descending the ladder leading from the helicopter to the ground. This, of course, made me cry, which made my mom yell louder, which made me cry harder. When my mother screamed she would scrunch up her face, set her jaw like a vice grip and she looked like she might explode. I was terrified of her and even more terrified that I might miss Santa. That is very scary for a four year old. As I relived this event, I felt sad for the little girl of me. Though I understand now how difficult it must have been for my mother to get five children dressed and out the door in time for an event, this incident was "fearful" for the four-year-old me.

I'm sure this affected me then, but it didn't define who I am and who I became. So, I decided to fast forward to a more joyful experience when I was nine years old and living in Munich, Germany.

We moved to Frankfurt, Germany in 1958 and then to Munich one year later. Even though I was young, I remember feeling heaviness in Munich. As an adult, I realize that even though it was thirteen years after the Second World War and the Holocaust, those energies lingered in the land and among the people. I will never forget going to Dachau with my parents. Even as a child, I felt something dark had happened there. This darkness seemed to creep into my body because I immediately became ill. I remember overhearing my parents discussing whether I had been too sensitive for Dachau. Then, again, when I was twenty-three, I returned to Dachau with friends who felt compelled to learn of the Holocaust first hand. I was again sick in bed for a week, my body reacting to what could not be spoken or understood.

One day, I won a bet with my brother Dick and I was rewarded with a coveted trip to his private hideaway where all the heaviness of the city disappeared. His hideaway was called, "Little Paradise."

The next morning we got up early and set out on our bikes. It was a perfect Saturday morning with the sun shining brightly. Although my brother feigned anger, I believe he was secretly proud to show me his special place. I was proud of myself for keeping up with my older, stronger brother. We cut through our neighborhood and headed left leaving behind all that was familiar and American. We cycled through many local neighborhoods with beautifully maintained apartment buildings, all with a generous display of flowers hanging over the balconies. I don't know a lot about flowers but when they are done well, with an artist's touch, the result is magical. The flower boxes were full of multi-colored flowers that I would say were pansies. The front of the apartment buildings started with short flowers gaining height as they worked there way toward the surface of the building – roses, peonies, and day lilies. Each change in flower was accompanied with a change in color – reds, pinks and yellow. The natural beauty of those homes stuck with me even all these years later.

As we continued our trek, we cut through residential neighborhoods with women sweeping the sidewalks in front of their homes. Germans were meticulous about their homes – every house was tidy and the gardens were organized according to shades and richness of color. Soon we passed an industrial area and cut through the back alley onto a major road. I wondered if my brother was playing a trick on me because it was so far away. I was peddling as fast as I could, and I was getting tired, and my legs were wobbly, but I pressed on. Finally, we came to a much less populated area. The slight wind carried the sweet smell of flowers and I realized we had left the city behind. I was hopeful that we were getting closer but I didn't dare ask my brother for fear he would think I was a sissy. We began a steady climb along the railroad track. The grass looked iridescent green in the suns light and the sky looked like a holy card sky: so blue with those fluffy white clouds filtering down a single perfect ray of sunshine on the saint below. My anticipation grew. Finally, my brother turned around on his bike and grinning from ear to ear asked if I was ready. I could hardly stand the excitement as I nodded. He yelled, "Hold on tight," as he made a sharp right turn down the steep hill and through a tunnel connecting to the valley below. We went up another big hill and there at the top was the most beautiful sight I had ever seen. My brother stood beside me, straddling his bike, with the proudest smile spread across his face while I leaned into my handlebars, panting and speechless. In front of me lay acres of lush, green fertile land bordered by a river on the left and a dense forest on the right. About two thirds of the way across, the river turned right toward the forest and became a path through the woods. Throughout the rolling hills were groves of trees and large boulders that were perfect for climbing and jumping. One of the larger trees had a tire swing hanging from it. At the far end was a long bridge running perpendicular to where the railroad crossed back over. I prayed silently that I would remember how to get back to this extraordinary place. Then, my brother took off down the hill.

This became my place where everything was always perfect. The darkest mood, the saddest day, the oppressive heat and energy of the city all disappeared here in Paradise. And I shared it only with my best friend Bo-bo. We did everything together, Bo-bo and me. His mother died when he was ten and we lived in the same apartment building in Munich, one floor apart. I remember the big upset when Bo-bo gave me his mother's wedding ring and asked me to marry him. I giggle now remembering how one neighbor told another until finally my mother got wind of it and asked me if it was true. "Yes," I said, as I showed my mother my sparkling diamond ring that was wrapped with a wad of tape so it would fit and announced, "now we're married!" Then came her long, sweet explanation of why I had to give the ring back; I was simply too young to be married and Bo-bo's father would want to keep that ring to remind him of his beloved wife who had passed away. That explanation made perfect sense to me so I gave it back – married less than twenty-four hours at the age of nine!

Bo-bo and I were always in some sort of trouble but it usually wasn't our fault. I remember the incident on the stairway of the apartment building when the wicked upstairs neighbor, Mrs. Benary, was screaming at Bo-bo for making too much noise in the stairwell. I quickly ran to get my mother who was one of those Irish Moms – you don't ever mess with her children, and since his mother's death, Bo-bo became her child, too. She came out of our apartment, running up the stairs two at a time to the landing where Mrs. Benary stood with Bo-bo. Mom told all of us children to go back to our house and have some cookies and milk while she spoke with Mrs. Benary. We pretended to leave, even slammed the door to our house, but then hid quietly in the stairwell to listen in on their conversation. My mother began calmly by telling Mrs. Benary that young Bo-bo was her responsibility now that her best friend had died; that if she had a problem with him to come to her. Then her Irish temper exploded and she began yelling about showing a little heart and what the hell was wrong with her anyway, and couldn't she see how the boy was suffering, and what difference did a little noise in the stairwell make. Huddled under the staircase, the five of us were torn between laughter, astonishment, and righteous indignation. The next morning mother came to the breakfast table with a bruise the size of an orange on her chest where she, agitated and animated, had pointed to herself, then to Mrs. Benary, than back to herself as she defended Bo-bo. She had so ferociously punctuated each sentence with her deadly pointer finger until she created a hematoma on her chest! My dad and all of us kids laughed hysterically when Mom showed us her battle scar. I'm smiling now because I realize I have become an equally fiercely protective mother.

On the way home from "Little Paradise," we stopped at my brother's favorite kiosk and bought a funnel full of candy. The owner of the kiosk tore off the paper from the roll, twisted it into a funnel and began filling it with all the delectable confections that my brother pointed to; all this for just twenty phenning which was equivalent to about fifteen cents in those days. We sat on the bench and gorged ourselves, aware even at that young age, that this day had been perfect: the love of two siblings, the sweet vibrations of nature, not to mention – all those delicious sugary confections. We were in heaven.

I think our experiences of heaven see us through the hellish times. It is the contrast that keeps us awake and engaged. In Germany, only miles apart, were the hell of the Holocaust and the beauty of paradise. Similarly, in the natural world, I have experienced the fear and awe of a powerful and devastating hurricane, only to have my heart break open with the shimmering iridescent blues, reds, greens and yellows of the rainbow that followed.

Sometimes embracing the "hell" in our lives brings us, indirectly, to heaven. It's similar to holding a yoga posture. First it is uncomfortable and your mind says, "I don't even like yoga, what am I doing here?" Then, the discomfort becomes pain but your mind reminds you: you're in class and you don't want to drop the pose so you stick it out. Absorbed in the breath, the mind turns off, the heart opens, and you relax into the pose and find comfort. Then you relax and breathe more deeply and, sometimes enter into bliss. I think that life is like that. Heaven and hell meld into one as we begin to see life with clear eyes. It's not important how difficult the yoga posture or the life is. It's about cultivating a firm mind and open heart and an eagerness to accept the challenge.

We are, of course, so different even in our similarities. How we react to bad news about our health has everything to do with how we have tended to react to anything unpleasant in the past. I saw a plethora of attitudes and behaviors surrounding difficult news about health in my chiropractic practice. Some people get angry and feel put out; others see it as a temporary set back that requires immediate attention; some embrace denial; and others let their illness become their life. I often found these people difficult to treat because they have given all their power and energy to their diagnosis. Yet, I understand that this is their own method of dealing with disaster and it keeps them in the game. I, too, reacted to my diagnosis of cancer in character: a mixture of heartbreaking disbelief, shock that threatened to cut off my air supply, innocence, disappointment, sadness, and then, much later, courage and gratitude. I allowed each emotion to fill me up, stay for a while and then pass through me because it was important to me to be honest and in the moment with each and every emotion. While I wasn't at all pleased with this new presence in my life, I still believe there are no mistakes, and that there was an opportunity here so I should pay attention.

A marvelous therapist and dear friend once suggested to me that I invite my hurts and sadness for a visit and a cup of tea to get acquainted and to have a conversation. Then, I asked the difficult questions that only this pain could answer: "Why are you here? How long have you been waiting for my attention? How can I benefit from this opportunity? What do you need to heal?" Simply asking pertinent questions and then listening with the ears of the heart to our soulful responses can help us to be in relationship to our particular pain; for our particular life. Pain and illness are deeply personal and provide opportunities to learn more about ourselves. Listening to what others say about our pain, like well meaning doctors can be meaningful too; however, it is our history that we bring to our wounds that make them uniquely ours. When we sit quietly with our pain, we honor our biochemical and spiritual individuality.

I can't say that I am always ready to hear the answers that I am seeking, nor am I always ready to act on those answers, but they are there for me when I am ready and willing. For me it has often been lonely listening to that inner voice because it is a lone voice in a field with hundreds of other, much louder voices telling me what I must do if I am to live. That voice, my inner voice, over the years has always been right for me, so it is very hard to ignore.

I have been deeply inspired by those patients who came to my office who had very little in life but who showed immense gratitude for what they had because they felt they had been singled out and blessed. One man in particular comes to mind. He had five children, two biological and three adopted. Four of his children were physically and emotionally challenged. When he described his mornings of getting all the children out of bed, fed, and off to school, it sounded like pure hell to me. For him, it was the best part of the day. He was so joyful and thanked God every morning for being so blessed. He truly believed he was a lucky man. And he was because he thought he was. "As a man thinketh in his heart, so is he." (Proverbs 23:7).

The flip side of being grateful is more prevalent in this country of immense affluence and entitlement. We often think we are missing something even though we have everything we could possibly want, or need. I have also encountered patients who experience overwhelming feelings of emptiness. I, too, experienced this sense of lack in my thirties and forties but I felt far too guilty to discuss it with anyone. I felt there was a hole in my soul and my spirit was slowly and painfully leaking out. I could not say why and I could not name a single thing in my life that was wrong. It was all right; it seemed perfect to me. I had crafted this life for myself but somewhere along the line I forgot to live it. The real me had checked out. I questioned whether this suffering even belonged to me. Perhaps I was suffering for the earth or the people of the earth. Was it possible that I agreed to receive collective pain, and, like a conduit, to pass it through myself down to the core of the earth where it could be burned and transformed? Sometimes it felt exactly like that but when I thought about it too hard, it seemed preposterous. I was relentless in my efforts to understand this experience. I spent many years digging into my psyche as if my life depended on it and it did. I knew that to be free, I would have to learn why I was caging myself; why I was disallowing happiness in my life. It is a process, this uncovering, and for me it was like an archeological dig – slow, patient, gentle, sometimes painful but always interesting, and a beautiful coming together of a life. I suspect this is where my idea of taking the wrong turn began, in this digging into the cracks and crevices, turns and straight-aways of my life looking for answers and hope.

Now, many years later, as I reflect on my childhood in Germany, I do remember sadness and loneliness but mostly I remember ages seven through twelve as good years with a lot of heady accomplishments: I could run faster than most of the boys, play baseball with the best of them, roll a tire just as fast, climb a tree faster and higher than most and keep up on my bike. These were the things that mattered most to me. I also knew that hanging out with the boys was coming to an end because they were beginning to feel that hanging out with girls was not at all cool. I ignored that chatter because there was nothing I would have rather been doing than playing hard outdoors.

I didn't have many girl friends; I found relationships with girls more challenging, especially with Christine who was a spoiled, only child but a friend nonetheless. She had a frightening and fiercely protective dog that was the more serious problem. This dog, whose name escapes me, had no redeeming qualities; he was hideous, anti-social, unkind and very territorial. He had short brown hair, close set eyes and looked like a cross between a vizsla and a pit bull. And, he only responded to German. His home was in the bathroom, next to the toilet. When I spent the night and I had to use the bathroom, which I almost always did, I would have to walk directly in front of this dog to get to the toilet. I lay in bed for what seemed like hours trying to talk myself out of needing to pee. When I couldn't hold it any longer, I would muster all the confidence I could to begin my walk down the hall to the bathroom. I would tell myself he is just a dog, he hasn't ever bitten a friend of Christine's and he is just warning me not to come too close. The minute I turned on the light to begin my long, arduous journey down the hall, he would hear me coming and begin his low, deep, menacing growl. Then, when he saw me he would bare his teeth, stare at me with that cold, deep stare that seemed to dare me to come closer. I absolutely hated this part of spending the night away from home but Christine was an only child, not one of five, and it was nice to have a change of pace from our hectic household. It was then that I would begin my chant, in German, for him to stay in his place, "Geh in dein Platz, geh in dein Platz." Finally, having accomplished my task, I would get back to bed in a full throttle episode – heart pounding, palms dripping with sweat and nausea – but I would feel oh so relieved that I was victorious again – I made it to the bathroom and back without being mauled. That dog and I never grew to like each other, we never came to an understanding, and we barely tolerated each other. But those trips to the bathroom toughened me up and I drew strength from that.

These simple accomplishments, physical and mental, cumulatively begin to shape who we are and who we become. Those were positive years for me and I didn't discover anything unhealthy lurking behind those tomboy years that may have come back to haunt me. I did not take a wrong turn during those early years from seven to twelve; I was developing in a true and authentic way. I did continue to feel more comfortable in male company than female company into my late 30's when motherhood completely changed the way I viewed woman. I was suddenly in awe of women; how we did so much and made it look so simple; how we popped out those babies and never missed a beat; how we struggled to juggle husbands, children, parents, career and household while taking care of ourselves with the veneer of ease and grace. But it isn't easy and I found sisterhood with like-minded women a great comfort.

We returned from Germany to the United States in 1965 and my siblings and I returned to Catholic School. This was important to my parents who believed we would grow up to become better human beings with stronger moral values with the sacred influence of the church and the rigorous teaching of the nuns. I had a healthy respect for the nuns; however, except for my older sister who was rather bookish at the time; my other three siblings and I were scared to death of them. I could never quite figure out if they were human, more than human, or far less than human. I leaned towards the latter. My simple, seventh grade assessment of these nuns was that they did not exercise their right to a diversity of choices when they joined the convent and that they were completely miserable and took it out on the students, especially those that seemed to be having the most fun.

Most of the diocesan elementary schools fed into one large Catholic high school called Denis J. O'Connell. The school acted like two separate schools: the boy's side, taught by Jesuit brothers, and the girl's side, taught by the Sacred Heart nuns. The only interaction, supposedly, was at lunchtime in the cafeteria. (Given that, I still have to wonder how so many girls got pregnant!) Now, I am a strong proponent of same sex education but I wanted all the benefits of that: rolling out of bed, throwing on a wrinkled uniform, brushing teeth, but little attention to hair, hygiene or make-up and just barely making it to class on time. However, when you throw in a common cafeteria and courtyard, bringing the boys and girls together at certain times of the day, it totally screws up the beauty of having no boys around because I still wanted to look my best and clearly all the other girls did, too. That meant still doing the make-up thing, rolling up the uniform at the waist to show a little leg (for which I received a multitude of detentions), and generally having radar for eligible, hunky, guys. The truth is that you can't separate male and female teenagers with raging hormones and burning curiosity no matter how hard you try.

In spite of the nuns and the boys on the other side of the wall, I found a nice rhythm at O'Connell High. I enjoyed friendships that I had cultivated since kindergarten and first grade prior to going to Germany, and then in seventh and eighth grade upon our return. I also enjoyed the challenging curriculum. But, in order for us to receive this great education, my mother had to drive two hours a day to the furthest bus stop still in the diocese. That ended after my freshman year because my older sister graduated, my brother pleaded to go to public school (he hated the intense discipline of Catholic school) and my mother finally had enough of chauffeuring us those great distances. While I was not looking forward to the transition to public school, sophomore year proved to be a good one.

In retrospect, I realize that fifteen is an auspicious time because it is the beginning of a new seven-year cycle. These seven-year cycles refer to our physical and psychological development as well as the rhythm and flow of evolving soul energy all of which seem to shift roughly every seven years. When I think of these spiritual growth cycles I imagine a chrysalis preparing to become a butterfly. It just lies there, upside down, hanging from a tree or bush, jammed into this tiny space, until finally you see movement and a pushing out from the inside. Something compelling is trying to bust out of there and become her true, exquisite self, and by doing so, becomes irrevocably larger and more beautiful than before. The chrysalis itself is not attractive; it is a holding place of rest and preparation, and an integral part of the transition from dark creepy crawly caterpillar to spectacular, vibrant colored butterfly. I love to think of myself breaking free, at all costs, determined to fly like the butterfly. And yet, I am clear that I have yet to do this as gracefully as the caterpillar. Instead of hiking into the woods and waiting there peacefully for metamorphosis, my transformation looks more like a child's temper tantrum: kicking and screaming, tears and angst, daring anyone to get in my way as I wait for this transition that I know is coming, better be coming soon, because I can't go on as I am; I must take flight! So, when I started my sophomore year, I couldn't wait to spread my wings.

I was trying to engage at Thomas Jefferson High School, the new public school I was attending, but it was difficult to find my rhythm. Nonetheless, I did make new friends, including a young man whose soul fit mine. I learned so much from him about love and respect, about honoring who each person is and making space for that person; I learned that I am not the least bit jealous (which can be interpreted as disinterest) and I learned that I had a deep fear of intimacy and of losing myself - my individuality - when in a relationship. It was a struggle for me to stay together but separate and yet it was a new, precious experience. I found a new appreciation for who I was as I saw myself through my sweetheart's eyes. I still appreciate that love and friendship because it served as a gauge for what is pure and healthy.

It was heartbreaking then, when we learned that my father was being transferred once again and that we would be moving to Taipei, Taiwan. I would begin my third high school in three years (there would be five by the time I graduated) at Taipei American School. Thankfully, Taiwan would be my dad's final tour of duty and our final uprooting.

CHAPTER THREE

Circling

*Do you love yourself enough
to listen with the ears of your heart
to the other voices of yourself speaking?*

Beno Kennedy

Our move to Taipei was different from previous tours of duty because, this time, one of us would stay behind. My sister Carolyn would stay in America at Mary Washington College. My brother would begin his senior year in Taipei and prepare for college back in the States and I would begin my junior year which was pivotal for me. I love adventure but as we pulled up to our new home, I was in culture shock – completely floored by the water buffalo grazing in the rice paddies - I'd never even heard of water buffalo! Our home was surrounded by a ten-foot high stone wall with rows of sharp, cut glass embedded along the top for security and protection. We also had a young Taiwanese couple living with us who were meant to keep us safe and guard our home, but instead, robbed us blind.

Having a live-in cook/butler and seamstress was my mother's undoing because they took over all of her daily tasks from which she had derived her primary sense of self for so many years. At my mother's urging, my father told his colleagues at CIA that he would like to let our help go. We were told, in no uncertain terms, that we would be courting disaster, for within hours it would be known among the locals that we had no one protecting our home and we would be continually at risk. That was the end of that and my mother reached an understanding with the Taiwanese couple that it was her kitchen, that she would be the main chef, but that she would be happy for them to serve breakfast and lunch. She would also sew in the sewing room on her own sewing machine when she felt inclined and she would do some of the marketing at the commissary. She took typing and art classes but all in all, she was miserable in Taiwan and all of us children were sensitive to that. Even as a young one, I had a sense that tending to my mother's happiness was my responsibility. Taipei was too primitive, too hot, and too confining for her and she couldn't find her rhythm, even among the American wives, some of whom she already knew from previous tours. I don't think she ever got used to walking into the kitchen at night, turning on the lights, and seeing huge, black, multi-legged cockroaches bouncing off the hard, shiny white porcelain surfaces of the kitchen and flying around her head. This, among other things, clawed at her sensibilities and contributed to her unhappiness.

I remember those little critters giving me the creeps too, but it simply came with the territory. Now I realize that often, when people reach midlife, we don't feel like playing by the rules anymore; we would rather take the ball and go home. In retrospect, I think my mom felt like that and, because of her health, we did eventually pack up the family and go home.

As a dependent teenager, I noticed as Americans in a foreign country, we stuck together, regardless of age, color, creed or appearance. I didn't find the cliquishness and occasional cruelty that is so prevalent among teenagers in the U.S. There wasn't a "cool" group or a "not so cool" group, there was just one group: the American youth. That, of course, made fitting in very easy and instantaneous. However, this tightly defined group was accompanied by very relaxed moral and ethical behavior - for many of the kids, drugs, alcohol and sex were part of the every day mix. It was not uncommon for students to be drunk or on drugs by 9:30 in the morning. Anything you could possibly want could be found on the streets for a negligible price - from pirated music to prostitution. For teens who were particularly adventuresome and who enjoyed flirting with the dark side, Taipei was nirvana.

I was not one of those kids, and it was at this juncture in my life that I became more discerning both socially and personally. I became clear about who I was and, more importantly, who I was not; what I could tolerate and what was unacceptable. Now, forty years later, I realize that I learned to be judgmental then, something that I struggle to tame even now.

My older brother Dick, who was 17 at the time, partnered with the dark side of life in Taiwan. He found great comfort, pleasure and escape in what the black market offered: drugs, alcohol and prostitution. He was later diagnosed with paranoid schizophrenia and I see now how his excessive use of drugs and erratic behavior was a prelude to his burgeoning illness. I adored Dick. He was an extremely bright and talented young man but his behavior was increasingly disturbing to me. In large families, it is common for parents to require the older children to look after the younger ones. Our family was no exception to this rule: we stuck together and kept tabs on one another. We were happy to do this because we enjoyed each other's company. Probably being uprooted every few years and moving to a different country contributed to our closeness because we depended on one another for entertainment and companionship. Our looking after one another freed up my parents to do other things and to look after the youngest; it also kept them blissfully ignorant of the destructive side of teenage behavior in Taipei. During that time my mother's midlife discontent and my father's concern that he had made a poor choice taking us to Taiwan kept them both preoccupied. I think they believed that if we left the house together and we returned home together, that we spent the time in between innocently having fun together. But that wasn't always the case.

I remember the particular night when being my brother's keeper wasn't fun anymore. After hanging out all evening, it was time to go home, but I couldn't find Dick. I finally found him at a brothel. It was close to eleven at night and I was cautiously walking down a very dark alley in an unfamiliar part of town trying to find my brother. The air was pungent with the smell of greasy dumplings, oppressive heat, sweat and hopelessness. I was dripping with fear so I began humming to myself (something I had done ever since watching Mary Martin in the "King and I" where she told her son that whenever he was afraid, to just whistle a happy tune). Finally, I saw familiar faces outside a doorway. Dick looked at me with a cocky smile that was a mixture of shame, pride, incredulity and amazement that I had come here alone to find him. I simply said, like a disappointed mother, "come on, it's time to go home."

Family systems therapy asserts that it is typical for one person in the family to manifest the dysfunction or illness of the whole family system. In that light, that person in our family was Dick. Up to that point in my life, I believed my family was perfect. And yet, I was aware that my mother was unhappy, my sister was alone in America, my brother was acting out and I was unable to fit in. Though I was only sixteen at the time, I was perceptive enough to know that something wasn't right; that life wasn't as sweet as it used to be. All my emotions were stirring inside me; I was confused and uncomfortable about what was "normal." Most of my peers were in agreement as to what was "fun"- alcohol, drugs, hooking up, skipping school, and generally pushing the margins for what was acceptable behavior for adolescents. I certainly wasn't a saint; I also wanted to have fun but it wasn't always about parties and alcohol. I was interested in learning about the

Taiwanese culture and countryside; I was president of a sorority whose main purpose was to raise money for charities and I enjoyed hanging out with my family. So, I concluded that I must be "abnormal." The truth is, I never really fit in as an adolescent but I was usually willing to try. However, that first year in Taiwan, I realized I had no desire to fit in. I wouldn't behave in a way that betrayed who I was. I was miserable.

I told my parents I wanted to move back to the states and live with my older sister in Fredericksburg while she attended Mary Washington College. I figured I would attend a local high school there. As the middle child, the peacemaker, who never rocked the boat, my parents were shocked. They said it was out of the questions – I was simply too young to be on my own. After considering some alternatives, we compromised and I enrolled in a Chinese parochial boarding school across the river.

Attending this school changed everything for me. I had exercised my voice and I had been heard. I drew strength from that victory as I prepared to enter yet another high school. I was both delighted and anxious about my new school situation because of the distance, the lack of familiarity of people and culture and also, being separated from my family. My Mom was heartbroken to let me go. It was doubly difficult when my younger sister, Judy, decided at the last minute that she wanted to go as well. Our leaving left my mother with her three girls away at school, a son who was descending into mental illness and a younger son of eleven at home.

Once I left what was American, I embraced everything Chinese. It was an awakening. I went from being a miserably unhappy child to a thriving young woman. At the International School, there were five American girls', as well as girls from the Philippines, Thailand, Japan, China and Taiwan. Because our class consisted of only eighteen students, we became very closely connected. We were a community and that felt good.

I am amused now as I reflect on returning to Virginia from Taiwan and the first time my friends and I went to a Chinese restaurant. We were talking, laughing and catching up. Suddenly, I noticed a deafening silence and as I looked up from my plate, there were five sets of eyes staring at me as though I was an alien. With a mouth full of noodles, most of which were dangling from my mouth, I asked, "what?" I realized that, with chopsticks in hand, I had been shoveling food into my mouth without coming up for air, and my friends were mortified! I started to laugh uncontrollably, unable to explain why because every time I looked at their incredulous faces, I started to laugh even harder. Then I started to choke, which only made matters worse. Finally, I explained that I was always hungry at boarding school because they didn't serve enough food. With six students to a table and eight portions in the center of that table, and only chopsticks to eat with, I learned to eat insanely fast so that I could be the first to reach for seconds. That night with my friends, I learned that it would be best if I didn't use chopsticks in public. Over the years, I have learned to tone it down, but I still have a propensity to shovel in the noodles when I have chopsticks in my hand. It's funny the things that stay with you; when I hold chopsticks, I'm hopelessly conditioned to start shoveling.

I found the Sacred Heart nuns in Taiwan to be far more humane than the Sacred Heart nuns that I experienced in the United States. Our Mother Superior was a marvelous character: warm, bright, and witty; and she always had a twinkle in her eye. We were convinced that she was having an affair with the papal nuncio, which we applauded. Our first clue was that she giggled. I had never actually seen a nun giggle. And she blushed, bright red, whenever they sat together during those rare occasions when he came to visit our school. Most importantly though, she disappeared for hours and sometimes days whenever he came to visit. You can imagine our vivid imaginations: eighteen horny adolescent girls living vicariously through, of all people, our Mother Superior. The stories got juicier with each week that we were separated from boys. In fact, the stories began to be more about us then Mother Superior, as our adolescent hormones raged. Sometimes I wondered about the two of them and hoped they were having as much fun as we imagined they were. Nonetheless, it was our Mother Superior's direction, sense of adventure and joi de vivre that was the driving force behind my love for my new school. I had found a comfortable niche in which to grow. My sister, Judy and I often came home on weekends to visit our family which thrilled my mother. She took great pride and enjoyment in cooking our favorite meals and the dinner table was full of excitement and stories. But it was clear that my mom was aching for her two girls and after a few months, we decided we would become part-time boarders.

This decision took my sister and me on an incredible adventure two mornings a week as we set out for school. Getting to school took almost two hours and involved walking, buses, ferries, and hitchhiking. At 5:30 a.m., at the foot of our street, Nanking Road, we literally fought our way onto the public bus. There was no guarantee that we would both get on with our limbs intact so we grabbed hands and held tightly as we fought our way on. The scene was complete and utter chaos. Early in the morning thousands of people used public transportation to get to work. We had never had an occasion to take public transportation prior to this because the State Department provided free transportation to all Americans to designated areas like the Post Office, Commissary, PX, teen center and school. We eventually became regulars on the Chinese bus and the locals began to look out for us, helping us on and off the bus and pushing people out of our way so that we could board. We laughed and thanked them, "xie xie ni" and they bowed and said, "bu kegi," You're welcome. Once, as we were boarding the bus, I felt my sister's grip on my hand loosen and her fingers slipped away. Our new friends on the bus, mostly older men and woman, stooped and toothless, eyes shining and grinning ear to ear, yelled at the bus driver in Taiwanese to stop and let the poor pathetic American girl off so she could go back and get her sister.

On our bus, people were hanging off the back and out the windows, women were holding babies, chickens, baskets of eggs, and ducks; and when there was absolutely no space left on the bus, another five people would get on. And the smell was perfectly reflective of the situation; it was a combination of dirty diapers on dirty children, barnyard animals, earthy soil and manure and poor hygiene. And that is how we began our school day.

Following our thirty-minute bus ride, we hiked to the ferry. I delighted in this part of the trip because of the slow pace of life and the rolling hills with the one lane dirt road that made its way through the beautiful countryside. While we waited for the lazy ferry to return to our side of the river, we purchased a typical Chinese breakfast of hardboiled eggs, rice and bread from one of the moveable noodle stands. The smell of those stands: hot grease, flour, pungent meat, fish, sweat and cigarette smoke, still stays with me today. It was a small ferry which only held a couple of motor bike drawn carts and a dozen or so people. The ride across the river took about thirty minutes and it was never crowded. This was the most relaxing and enjoyable part of the trip and we usually sat quietly, eating our breakfast and studying. Because Americans were such a novelty on this route, often times the locals would practice their

English with us and we usually ended up laughing and communicating with gestures and facial expressions. I came to love these people and their gentle ways, which is why I loved this commute. Once we arrived at the other side of the river, we hitchhiked the rest of the way. We were deep in the country now and there were no taxis or regular public transportation. When we saw a cart or trailer powered by oxen, horses, motorcycle, or motor bike coming down the road, we would begin running as fast as we could, back packs bouncing, out of breath and giggling uncontrollably, and we would do our best to jump on board. If one of us didn't make it, the other one jumped off and we waited for the next opportunity. I can't say that the local merchants were happy to have the additional weight of two foreign teenagers on board, but they tolerated us and we thanked them graciously sometimes with treats or money.

Getting to school on time was challenging but it was also a great adventure. What I found most exhilarating about our commute was learning about the people, the culture and the country. That could never have happened if I had stayed at the American school and associated only with the other military children. Naturally introverted and contemplative, I found that countryside and the river calmed my soul. That still happens today when I am in the mountains or swimming in a mountain lake.

Many years later, when I began searching for something that would plug up the hole in my soul, I remember describing this adventure to a therapist who said, with immense gravity and some repugnance, "Jacqui, in my world, that's called child abuse." I disagreed. For me, it was a brilliant opportunity to use my ingenuity, strength, intelligence, wiles, time management and physical endurance to accomplish my goal: keeping us all happy.

Our great adventure in traveling back and forth to school came to an abrupt end just before Christmas. My mother's heart was still broken and she had a stroke, so we had to take her back to the United States for medical care. Perhaps it was the heartbreak of my brother's continued downward spiral, or her ill-fit in Taiwan; perhaps it was her loneliness for her three daughters away at school or the forced sharing of her household chores with two strangers; or maybe it was, as the doctors said, her smoking in conjunction with taking birth control pills that caused the stroke. Whatever the reason, it was very sad for all of us; each of us had to deal with our own personal disappointments about leaving the Island, as well as our fear and concern for Mom.

Following her fifth child in eight years, my mother, a devout Catholic, had quietly decided to take birth control pills, directly opposing her Catholic Faith. She believed her stroke was punishment for her decision. My mother never returned to Church after that stroke. I think she felt that God had betrayed her. She did, however, recover almost one hundred percent which was a blessing.

My years in Taipei were formative years. I learned who I was; what made me happy and what made me sad; I learned that I could change a bad situation into a good one and that there is usually room for compromise without selling your soul. Those lessons have served me well. They are, in fact, the very same lessons that I was forced to re-visit when I was diagnosed with cancer thirty-five years later. It is amusing to me that I haven't changed much in all these years: I am still scrupulous, somewhat inflexible, determined, intelligent, selective of the company that I keep, adventurous, and often lonely. I still don't always fit in and don't always care to. I still feel down sometimes, up more often, but generally appreciate life and see our connection to one another and to all that is. I am no longer religious, like I was then, but I do have a deep and rich spiritual life which sustains me and I almost always feel infinitely blessed when I see life through the eyes of my heart. Life does circle around and I can say with an open heart that I did not take a wrong turn or a short cut, nor did I take a pass on what life was offering me during my adolescence in Taiwan. I am grateful for this and how those early years have helped to shape who I am today.

When we returned to America, I changed high schools for the fifth and final time and began to think about college. My brother, Dick, who was attending Wheeling College, a small Jesuit college in West Virginia, dropped out the week before finals in a full schizophrenic episode. He hitchhiked home, came directly to my school and pulled me out of class to tell me before he told my parents. He was looking for approval, I was trying to understand, but all I could muster as I stood there in the front office, completely befuddled, was a surprisingly firm, "Go home and wait for me to come home." Dick was diagnosed with paranoid schizophrenia two week later.

Over the years, I have pondered this disease, schizophrenia. I have looked at it from different perspectives: medical, psychiatric, nutritional, chemical, alternative and energetic. It is a devastating mental illness. Not enough research has been made into developing greater understanding and better treatments for this illness. It is largely agreed that it is an interaction of genetics and environment, leading to brain dysfunction. There is also agreement that there is a chemical component. I also think there is a familial component, a behavior that is passed down in the family through the generations. Sometimes it is a subtle energetic that pushes someone over the edge. There appears to be a schism between what has been declared reality by society and what actual reality seems to be as is witnessed and understood by extremely sensitive and often gifted children. There also appears to be oedipal confusion that comes to bear on this and perhaps other sexual traumas, as well as confusion of the role that the child plays in the family: is he or she the son, daughter, father, lover, protector, important person or not so important person? The child's role could change suddenly and dramatically depending on whether it is in relationship to the dominant parent in the child's life or the less dominant parent. For example, if the child is the mother's favorite person in the family, even more loved than the husband, this would be a role enjoyed with regard to the mother but the father's resentment may border on dislike or distrust and not be comfortable for the child. How long this confusion of roles is allowed to go on and at what stage of development it ends also seems relevant. These are simply my observations over the years of patients I have seen with schizophrenia and my hope is that we will have greater understanding of this illness in the future.

Schizophrenia not only affects the sufferer; it affects the entire family. We all suffered in our own way, but no one as much as my mother. I can't imagine the heartbreak of watching your own child, who you love with all your heart, have his wings clipped just as he is taking flight; all the promise and possibilities ripped out from under him. My brother has been treated with anti-psychotic drugs for the last forty years, which comes with a lot of secondary symptoms, but these drugs have kept him functional.

CHAPTER FOUR

Breaking away

This being human is a guest-house
Every morning a new arrival.

A joy, a depression, meanness,
some momentary awareness comes
as an unexpected visitor.

Welcome and entertain them all!
Even if they're a crowd of sorrows,
who violently sweep your house
empty of its furniture.

Still, treat each guest honorably.
He may be clearing you
out for some new delight.

The dark thought, the shame, the malice,
meet them at the door laughing,
and invite them in.

Be grateful for whoever comes,
because each has been sent
as a guide from beyond.

Rumi

The 70's were a tumultuous time in America: the Vietnam Conflict (it was never declared a war) was still in progress; there was gross civil unrest; students everywhere were protesting the war and college campuses were full of students avoiding the draft. It was a paradoxical time of both/and: love/hate, hope/hopelessness, accomplishments/inertia, agitation/passivity. For many, it was also a time of immense disappointment and frustration with life as it was unfolding; a life that looked very different from the one we were raised to expect. Baby boomers everywhere were full of righteous indignation; it was in our music, our protests, and the general mood of the country.

In 1973, I attended graduate school for my Master's in Social Work. Like everyone else I knew then, I had no idea what I wanted to do with my life. Since my undergraduate degree was in Sociology, a MSW seemed to be a natural progression. It fit with my naive desire to change the world, or at least, to make a difference. The particular curriculum at Virginia Commonwealth University in Richmond, Virginia required you to be in class three days a week and externship two and a half days a week. My externship was in Staunton, Virginia about three hours from Richmond.

There - at Western States Mental Hospital - I met my match. Ms. Bone was the supervisor for the social workers on staff, including the interns. She was a Smith graduate, very bright, and always on task. We joked that when God was giving out hearts, He mistakenly gave

Ms. Bone testicles, and when Buddha was teaching about compassion, he illustrated its antithesis with a picture of Ms. Bone. Known as the "ice queen," her critiques of her students were never complimentary.

We had our own caseload and my patients included aging recidivists and teenagers. Many of the older patients had experienced multiple shock treatments and some had received frontal lobotomies. I believed this to be the most barbaric surgery performed on humankind under the auspices of scientific advancement. In this procedure the frontal or pre-frontal cortex, and/or the pathways leading to it, is removed. This area of the brain is responsible for such things as recognizing consequences for behavior, choosing between good and bad, suppressing bad behavior, realizing similarities between things and events, and remembering memories that are associated with emotions. The hope is that the frontal lobotomy will remove the problem behaviors. Lobotomy was used to treat many mental illnesses such as schizophrenia, clinical depression and anxiety disorders. In effect, it left the patient in a persistent semi-vegetative state. I agree with Norbert Wiener, the author of Cybernetics, in his assessment of this surgery: "prefrontal lobotomy . . . has recently been having a certain vogue, probably not unconnected with the fact that it makes the custodial care of many patients easier. Let me remark in passing that killing them makes their custodial care still easier."

During my externship, I found that the patients I treated shared one main characteristic: loneliness. They were starved for attention and human kindness. As a highly sensitive twenty-one year old, I found that when I was working there, I, too, felt lonely.

As the year drew to an end, the interns took their turn going before Ms. Bone for an evaluation and recommendation. I began thinking about that about a week before finals. I believed I had done as good a job as anyone could with mentally challenged, frontal lobotomy, and shock treatment patients. And I felt that I had actually worked quite well with the teenagers who responded beautifully to talk therapy. The staff acknowledged that there was less acting-out and fewer fights on the ward. I took that as a positive reflection of my work.

When the day arrived for my evaluation, I was the first intern to see the ice-queen. Things seemed to be going well as we went through each person on my caseload. Mostly, I spoke and Ms. Bone listened. Finally she looked up at me and said, with all the compassion of a robot: "Jacqui, you remind me of a "Suzie saccharin social worker" and I think you should get some life experience before you consider a career as a psychiatric social worker."

I was blind-sided and devastated and wished I could bi-locate back to my room like some of the shaman I had been reading about. Instead, feeling deeply embarrassed, I managed to say, in a quivering voice:

"I really don't know what you mean by that remark." And she replied,

"I think you know exactly what I mean, and if, after you think about it for awhile, you don't get it, come back and we'll talk."

I had never felt so hopelessly dejected, so completely wiped out in a way that I felt my insides melting away. And nobody had ever talked to me like that, which is a shame because my precious soul needed a little practice in dealing with that kind of honesty. I wasn't offended by Ms. Bone's pointing out my lack of life experience – she was right! – But, I was taken aback by her disdain for my unwavering optimism, albeit naïve at the time.

Today, thirty years later, I am still optimistic. It is a choice and I choose to see the glass half-full. It was Ms. Bone's perception that my sweetness was "synthetic" that stirred me up inside. I didn't think I was fake or toxic like saccharin. I was inexperienced and overcompensating for that lack. Probably I was too bubbly but I was twenty-one years old and it was my way of coping with all that misery. Couldn't she see that! I flew back to the intern's dorm where I had lived every Wednesday through Saturday for the past year, threw myself on my bed, and wept uncontrollably for hours. The rub was, I respected Ms. Bone's expertise so it took awhile to get my head around the incomprehensible.

She was right. I was too sweet and I could see how this could be perceived as inauthentic. I was caught up in my youthful need to receive approval and be liked. And I wasn't completely devoted to the profession, which

Ms. Bone sensed. While her harsh honesty shook me to the core, I was deeply appreciative of the bittersweet lesson which was pivotal for me: I did not have to get down in the trenches to feel like I was making a contribution to society and just because my brother was diagnosed with mental illness, I did not have to choose that path to help others like him. And I realized that work should be fun and fulfilling; it should not make me sad and lonely. So often in life, it is these heart-wrenching gifts that are dropped in our laps that offer us the greatest opportunity for growth and understanding. Ms. Bone did me a favor. My journey by-passed that turn towards social work in the early 70's and I have never looked back.

Coincidentally, when Ashley returned to the intern's dorm, I learned that she had been told essentially the same thing. And that is how it came to pass that the two of us, needing to "toughen up," decided to go hitch-hiking and back-packing through Great Britain, Europe, Africa and Israel for two years. I did pass my externship evaluation, however, I chose to defer the completion of my MSW, and instead took on three jobs to save money for our trip. This is my way – when one thing gets me down, I switch to something else that will renew me.

Reminiscing about this now, thirty years later, I am amused at Ms. Bone's foresight; she knew what she was talking about. My traveling years were transformational: I learned to listen to my inner voice, to appreciate nature and how it spoke to me, to see all things, all people as the same – One Heart, One Soul, One Breath; I began to understand the Oneness of life and the Divine and how it works in our lives if we allow it to.

Still, today, whenever life gets too intense, I have this recurring dream of me traveling in Europe: I am walking along a meandering river, with a blue mid-size pack on my back; I am wearing low, brown leather hiking boots, beige shorts and a light blue denim shirt; I am squinting into the bright morning sun and breathing in the violet-blue sky as I skip along from stone to stone; it's late spring or early summer. There is a small boulder the size of a large grapefruit tumbling through the swift current a few feet ahead of me. I feel this intense longing for something simple and carefree. Sometimes the longing is so intense, it wakes me up. It is a longing for those simple, joyful, youthful days when there are no plans, no responsibilities, no sense of what the day will bring, but complete surrender to whatever comes my way.

Over the years, I erroneously came to believe that my present life and those carefree days of traveling were mutually exclusive; that I couldn't have both; that I was a grown-up now and had to behave responsibly. So now, many years later, I am undoing those beliefs.

While I was traveling, I lived in the moment, fully experiencing new places, people, food, feelings, sites, sunsets, attitudes and our glorious natural world. I loved learning about and preparing for each new country by reading books (in the spirit of keeping the weight of our backpacks to a minimum, many of us would tear the heavier books in half, like James Michener's, *The Sun Also Rises,* and swap with one another), studying maps and learning basic language skills. While it seemed effortless at the time, these experiences had a profound effect on building my confidence and self-assurance. Each day I was tackling new tasks: learning about currency, language, customs, being respectful of ethics and morals of different countries, navigating travel by road, boat and rail, finding the least expensive place to eat and stay when we were not camping, and in certain countries, haggling for all purchases. In my youth and naiveté, I believed that Americans were loved throughout the world, but in many countries and among some people, there existed anti-American feelings. I learned not to engage with these feelings. I found, instead, that being cordial and respectful was the best antidote.

These small daily tasks went a long way towards shaping my identity as a confident and capable young woman, and that is how I returned to American in 1976. I was changed.

I have often asked myself, what I was really looking for when I decided, with Ashley, to go on that road trip. I knew it wasn't simply my reaction to Ms. Bone. While I was traveling, I was un-entangled, self-sufficient, and enjoying the process of growing. But mostly, I was on my own. As the middle child of five, I was deeply entrenched in our family dynamic. My mother saw to it that we were "tightly-knit" and that we didn't let others break into the nucleus of the family. She also made it difficult to break out of that nucleus. Later, when I was studying child development, I realized I wasn't clear where I began and my family ended. While this closeness was a great comfort to me long into my late teens, it took my trip around the world for two years to help me begin to extricate myself from the tight grip of my family.

I remember when my older sister, Carolyn, decided that she wanted to do the same thing. She and a friend were going to come to Europe, but her friend backed out at the last minute. Carolyn wrote and asked if she could come and travel with Ashley and me. I knew that would be like being back home taking care of things, so I said no. My family was incredulous at my refusal and it would be two years before my sister spoke to me again, but I had made my point and stood my ground. I was finally breaking free.

CHAPTER FIVE

Life Experience

Once the soul awakens, the search begins and you can never go back. From then on, you are inflamed with a special longing that will never again let you linger in the lowlands of complacency and partial fulfillment. The eternal makes you urgent. You are loathe to let compromise or the threat of danger hold you back from striving toward the summit of fulfillment.

Anam Cara by John O'Donohue

Like a miner panning for gold - but in my case looking for some sign of a wrong turn or missed opportunity - I continued to sort out the significant parts of my trip.

When we arrived in England, Ashley and I immediately cashed in our Britrail and Eurail pass as to join countless others in the age-old adventure of hitchhiking. Ashley was also twenty-three and her roots were in Rochester, New York. She had spent a semester in London when she was an undergraduate student a couple of years earlier so she was more familiar with the mass transit system, the interesting places to visit and how to find free or inexpensive tickets to concerts, theatre and live readings. She was also an expert at softening that crusty British exterior, which proved to be a blessing. We had very similar personalities and were respectful of one another's differences, so our friendship worked great. We looked after each other and took turns being the cheerleader when things didn't go our way. Ashley was an absolute joy as a traveling companion. She has continued to travel, learn, and educate through her work as a producer of cutting edge documentaries.

Hitchhiking was a marvelous means of moving about the country. In England, it was as civilized as "queuing up." On the exit ramps, young travelers lined up single file, destination signs held high, waiting to be picked up. It was effortless, cost effective and very safe. And it was always an advantage to be a woman - at least that is what we were told by the male travelers. Therefore, in an effort towards equanimity, if two young men were going the same place as we were, we would invite them to join us.

We had one horrific experience while hitchhiking in Rome when an exquisitely dressed, perfectly coiffed, white haired gentleman, driving a red Alfa Romeo, picked us up. Five minutes into the ride, he slowed down, pointed to his red indicator light and gestured for us to get out and push. Against our better judgment (which got substantially better after that incident!) we got out to push and the man drove away with everything we owned. I foolishly held on to the door as he pulled away until my legs began dangling in the air, while Ashley yelled, "let go Jacqui, let go." I ultimately let go and fell to the ground. As I hit the ground, I felt overwhelmed by a soupy mix of emotions: frustration, anger, violation but mostly indignation. The police later told us that this "debonair gentleman" was part of an organized crime ring whose purpose was stealing American passports. Ironically, on a hunch, we had put our passports down our pants that morning before setting out to travel. Nonetheless, we had a horrendous day of running around to set things right: the police station, the American embassy, and American Express office. That night, back at the youth hostel, the residents took up a collection and we were more or less back in business with everything we needed from toothbrush to underwear.

We were deeply moved by this outpouring of generosity and concern. It seems we had found a family of like-minded travelers. Their kindness softened the blow of the robbery and we moved forward. In fact, everything was replaceable except our most valuable possessions – our photographs and our journals. That was the most heartbreaking loss. So I made a commitment to myself that I would practice being as attentive as I could to what was happening moment to moment.

I was raised Catholic and I thought that seeing the Pope and receiving his blessing was tantamount to reaching nirvana. Unfortunately, our stay in Rome was cut short. After straightening out our business, Ashley and I decided to walk from the train station towards the Vatican. As we were strolling down the street, taking in the energy and activity surrounding us, including the colorful mix of flowers lining the Spanish stairs, a man came towards us, opened his dark trench coat, and with a twisted glint in his eyes, stood before us wearing only a smile. That, coupled with the previous day's events, was too much for us and we fled from Rome. I struggled to reconcile how, in what I was raised to believe was the holiest place in the world, these awful things could happen. I don't think, at that time, that my Catholic faith gave me what I needed to understand life's hurts and traumas. I wasn't mature enough or experienced enough to embrace the mystery and to know that there is always a silver lining; an inherent opportunity that can be teased out of the darkness. This has come with time.

We headed south to the Amalfi Coast where soaring mountains dropped dramatically towards the quiet fishing villages that dot the coastline. As far as you could see, fishermen were busy pulling in their catches for the day. It has been said that the Amalfi Coast was named after a gorgeous nymph who captured the heart of the famous god, Hercules. It is a breathtaking marriage of nature and environment: the pure white sand, the blue sky opposite the indigo waters of the Sea, and the small fishing boats rocking gently in the harbors. People were friendly but unfamiliar with American visitors. Thirty-five years ago, the Amalfi Coast was less traveled than today and we fell in love with its timeless charm.

We reluctantly left the beauty of the Amalfi Coast with the intention to sail to Tunisia to meet my friend who was doing research for his PhD. He offered to show us around. We arrived too late in Palermo to catch the daily shuttle across to Tunisia so we spent the night in a little pension across from the train station. During dinner I was aware of two rough looking men watching us. I wasn't particularly concerned but I couldn't shake the feeling that they were following us when we walked back to the pension. I told Ashley we should sleep in our clothes and have our backpacks ready to go just in case. Soon, we heard men's voices out in the hall. Then the twisting of the doorknob, which we had locked and secured with a chair pushed up against it. We jumped up, grabbed our backpacks and quickly climbed out the window. We flew down the rickety, old, black metal fire escape and ran across the slippery coble stone street to the railroad terminal. From there we could see the window from which we had just escaped and there were the two men from dinner, standing on the balcony looking down at us. Though by far the creepiest part of our trip, we were safe and protected. I was becoming increasingly conscious of what I perceived as spiritual protection and guidance which became more palpable during my travels, but which has always been with me. I was walking much closer to the edge, without a family net and I was profoundly grateful for divine presence.

Those feelings of being completely protected and held thirty-five years ago were very similar to my experience during my first diagnosis and subsequent treatment of breast cancer. I relinquished my hold on things and let go; I remembered that I am not in control, not even a little, and I completely surrendered. There is sublime sweetness in this middle ground of surrender and I did not want to leave it. I didn't understand then that it is not either/or but rather both/and. These ecstatic places where we exist from time to time are part of us, not separate from us, and we can simply invite them in. For the ten months after surgery, I surrendered and let myself be held and protected, and I experienced supreme peace and healing.

With the incidents of Italy and Sicily duly registered under "life experience," Ashley and I departed for Africa. Our plan was to cross northern Africa, from east to west, going as far south as the northern tip of the Sahara desert. We were blessed to meet two French speaking Swiss men, traveling in a Volkswagen van, on the boat over to Tunisia who planned this same trip. We arranged to meet them the week after our visit to Tunisia and embark on a two-month trek across Africa. We had been told that it was safer to travel with men in Africa because American women had a reputation for being fun, crazy and promiscuous. That is why we were especially thankful for our new traveling companions for making this trip possible.

This is often how things unfolded for Ashley and I: we fantasized about how we wanted the next month or two to unfold, we hoped and prayed for it and then let it go, and it usually came to us. It was magical. I often think back to that time and wonder what made that time so euphoric. Maybe, it was the sweetness of youth, our faith in good that had only begun to be tested, our trust in humankind and the fact that we made no real investment in the outcome. Whatever it was, it worked. I have tried to recapture that magic formula as I have matured, but it has required such an effort. Paradoxically, I am learning that when I give up trying and quiet myself down, life flows effortlessly.

Rolf and Karl, our new traveling companions, brought a trunk chock full of garments and treasures because they loved to trade at the markets. Trading was an art form which involved many cups of terribly strong, sweet tea, a smoking pipe of strong tobacco, and animated haggling. Since they both spoke French, and French is the second language in northern Africa, communication was not a problem. The process of making a purchase and/or a trade was fascinating to me and I learned a lot about culture, personality and the art of being gracious.

I particularly loved the markets in Morocco. Fresh vegetables, fruits, seeds, nuts and fresh herbs were colorfully displayed on shelves that were fashioned from the ground upwards. The exotic smells of herbs, fruits, flowers, and incense wafted through the humid air and stirred my senses as each stall I passed drew me in and captured my fascination. There were brightly woven blankets and baskets, engraved silver and brass, woodcarvings and more. There were thousands of people meandering through the market, some purposefully and others aimlessly. The market was the lively hub of a large, festive community.

One particular day, the festive nature of the market was subdued: a hungry woman had stolen a piece of fruit. There was so much commotion, that I was unable to grasp what had transpired. Then the crowd started running after this woman throwing stones. Rolf and Karl, who were much taller than Ashley and I, explained that the law of the street was Hammarabi's law – an eye for an eye and a tooth for a tooth. The thief not only had her hand cut off but she was also stoned by the crowd. Mouth agape, unable to move, Ashley forcibly moved me along but I have never been able to forget that image.

Another sight that pulled at my heart while we were traveling in Africa was the ubiquitous black veil, the chador. In many of the Muslim countries in 1974, the chador covered the entire woman except for the tiniest triangular opening on one eye. I had never seen this before and it brought tears to my eyes. I felt a strong urge to coax these women out of their exile behind the veil. But I knew if I acted on my impulse, I would be the second woman stoned on the streets of Morocco that morning. Recently, I've learned more about the chador and its implications. In 2007, I spent a year studying at the Hartford Seminary, which has the largest Muslim/ Christian study program in America. There I came to know beautiful, bright, accomplished women who chose to wear the veil. For them, it was a personal choice based on modesty and respect. Of course there are Muslim countries that still mandate wearing the veil.

I saw women in chadors in other countries but traveling through northern Africa was my first encounter with a blatant inequality between men and women. By comparison, it is understandable why American women wearing cut offs and tank tops, casually moving about their country, would be seen as prostitutes. Ashley and I felt blessed to be traveling through this part of the world with two men who kept us in their sight in public places; otherwise, we'd have been groped and grabbed. But it was those chadors that grabbed hold of my psyche in an inexplicable way, appearing in my dreams/ nightmares for years to come.

We were extremely cautious about what we ate and drank throughout our travels in Africa. Rolf and Karl did all the marketing and we cooked on the stove in the van. We treated all the water we bought and scrubbed fruit and vegetables with that water. One very hot and dry day, we stopped in a village along the way for ice cream. Since it was a national brand, we determined it would be safe to eat. It wasn't, we all contracted dysentery which lasted three weeks. I was hit the worst and we all thought that I might die. I have no recollection of the first five days and over the next week I continued to go in and out of consciousness. When it was over, I was emaciated.

Once we were all feeling well, we crossed the Atlas Mountains which span across Tunisia, Algeria, and Morocco. When the sun shines just right across these mountains, they turn a glowing magenta. It is breathtaking! I remember this part of the trip as being very serene, because of the majesty of this landscape and because there were few signs of humans. We crossed paths with Bedouins along our way and I was intrigued by the differences in how each tribe looked and dressed.

I have always been fascinated by how beauty is defined throughout the world. In America, we honor thinness. In Turkey, our lovely, corpulent friend, who traveled with us for six weeks, had a posse of men following her everywhere with complete and absolute devotion. In some cultures, corpulence is a sign of prosperity and considered incredibly attractive. When I lived in China during High School, the wealthy bound their feet, which was a sign of wealth and position. Here, in the Sahara, many of the women we saw wore countless brass rings around their necks to elongate them. Unnaturally long necks were considered beautiful, as were the bones and rings these women put through their lips, ears, and noses. In other parts of Africa, where the women wore clothes, their dress was very bright and colorful and I found them breathtakingly beautiful.

I find myself reflecting on going through chemotherapy and losing weight and all my hair, and how so many people told me I had never looked more beautiful. I understand they were being gracious, and I really appreciated that, but I sense it had to do with something else. True beauty comes when we allow our inner light to shine through. This inner light, in turn, comes from being at peace, feeling complete, being with God. That is how I felt during my treatment and that is what was shining through. I saw that same kind of beauty in the eyes and faces of the Bedouin women in Africa, and many years later, in the faces of the women of Tibet.

Our months in Africa passed quickly and the time had come for the four of us to go our separate ways: Ashley and I were heading to Spain for the running of the Bulls, and Rolf and Karl were making their way back home to Switzerland. We had become a family, the four of us, and had been through so much together that it was difficult to say good-bye. We knew that we would probably never see each other again. Ashley and I were feeling sad and lonely as we set up our campsite and settled in for the night. The next morning, as we sat eating breakfast, I watched Ashley's eyes grow big as saucers and a huge smile break across her face as she looked beyond my left shoulder. I turned to see Rolf and Karl walking towards us. They had missed us too. We spent one last unexpected day together which was a brilliant ending to our Africa adventure.

We traveled for two years, working a few months and traveling a few months. We chose to work where we wanted to stay, like UberLech in Austria where we worked in exchange for room and board and unlimited skiing! We did the same in Garmisch, Germany. We went to Pamplona, Spain for the running of the bulls, spent Easter on the Greek Island of Santorini (purported to be the lost island of Atlantis), visited the Piazza San Marco in Venice; enjoyed skiing in Zurmat, Switzerland and Chamonix, France; feasted at the Oktoberfest in Munich, Germany, did pub crawling in England and stood, stupefied, before the surreal beauty of the landscape of Scotland. We worked for many months on a Kibbutz in Israel and the more we saw, the more we felt we had to see for fear we would miss something. This wide world of ours began to feel more like a small community of friendly, supportive people. I think it's human nature that when we engage in an open, kind and gracious manner, the other person will usually respond in kind. We kept our hearts open and openheartedness came back. In this way, language was not a barrier.

I remember one icy cold winter morning as we were leaving the purple hue and steep pinnacles of the mountains of Switzerland to travel to Liechtenstein. We decided to stop for one last mug of steamy hot chocolate before we started hitchhiking. We were happy to postpone leaving one of our favorite countries and we thought we could spend the last of our Swiss francs. As we entered the café and grabbed a seat, Ashley and I emptied our pockets of all our coins and paper money and then studied the menu together, calculating exactly what to order so that we'd have no money left after we paid for our breakfast. When the waitress approached, we ordered something like one croissant and two cups of hot chocolate. A short while later, she brought us two full breakfasts and a pot of hot chocolate – on the house - she refused our money. I am sure that when she saw us, heads bent, studying the menu and counting out exact change, she assumed we could not afford a proper breakfast so she bought it for us. We were speechless and then began thanking her over and over again for her generosity. She just beamed; no words were necessary.

These selfless acts of kindness that we experienced were what made our traveling experience so remarkable.

It was the people, and our interaction and connection with them that was significant. I am convinced that kindness, open-heartedness, generosity, and a willingness to engage – is what contributes to health and well being. When I examine the times in my life that I have felt most content and have had a sense of belonging, I realize that it is when I have felt connected: connected to the life I am living, the people in my life and the natural world that surrounds me. This happened again and again in foreign countries, where I was separated from family and friends but very open and willing to engage (of course that was the purpose of the trip – to experience new places and people and to get "life experience"). My spirit likes to feel "connected" and I am at loose ends when I am not feeling that sense of belonging. I think we all are. Yet, when I was in Europe, even though I am a deeply private and protected person, I knew that I had nothing to lose by putting myself completely out there because I would never travel that same road again. And that is how it happened that in places that I had no connection whatsoever, I felt the most connected. It took me many years to understand this lesson and I still revisit it often – connection comes from the heart and a willingness to let others in. It is a choice and for some of us a difficult one.

Laughter also contributes to health and well-being. I remember reading about Norman Cousins who, when diagnosed with heart disease, rented a penthouse in New York City, played only funny movies (especially the Marx brothers), and allowed only people who could make him laugh, to come to visit him. He had researched the biochemistry of the brain and found that laughter was a great curative. Cousins claimed that he was cured of two separate illnesses because of laughter and a positive attitude.

I agree with Norman Cousins, laughter and fun are important. My daughter once told me that I didn't know how to have fun. Maybe she was right. I know I wasn't giggling a lot then because I was busy and overwhelmed and trying to hold it all together. Sometimes life is like that. And often the face of "fun" changes as we mature. We begin our career, start families and generally have more responsibility. For me, fun has become quieter, a subtle comfort inside that tells me things are good; life is flowing with ease.

Traipsing through Europe for two years was a blast in my twenties, but in my forties, being with my family and mothering, was my fun. Later though, when my children were teenagers and only tolerated their parents, mothering became more like policing. That's when I noticed I began running for my life, much like the bulls on the streets of Pamplona. I wasn't snorting or glistening with sweat, my eyes weren't bulging and I didn't appear frantic, but I was frantic and I was running.

Until recently, in my obsessive hunt for the wrong turn, I hadn't thought much about "connection" or "disconnection." What makes us feel "connected"? What gives us a sense of belonging? While in Europe, I felt deeply connected even though I was without family, on foreign soil, and had no routine, like work, to define me. I've come to understand that connection is not about what is outside of us; it has to do with the heart and how it opens and becomes a fertile garden in which to grow. I feel connected when I feel a divine presence in my life; it's like when the heart, soul, spirit and mind are lined up perfectly. I think that's what astrologers mean when they say your stars are lined up and you are going to have a good day. At these times in our lives we feel most alive; when we are undefended and trusting. I think that is when life truly happens; a healthy balanced life.

It is the opposite of connection or belonging that has caught my attention and is causing me deep concern. I believe that this scattered feeling, this discordant feeling underlies illness. It left a void in the center of me that was so empty that filling it seemed an insurmountable task. All the chocolate in the world couldn't fill it up and, believe me, I tried. We all choose our particular poison: alcohol, drugs, sex, extreme activities and exercise – but none of it works for long. As I walked through life, accumulating successes, I found it hard to remember when I got lost; when my heart stopped singing and went on "automatic." It is a slow process and it is cumulative but one day I woke up and realized something was terribly wrong. I don't think I am alone in this; it seems to be an epidemic in our country.

While I might not have wowed my supervisor during my externship, I did my "life experience" directive brilliantly. I learned so much more than books could ever have taught me and I better understood the subtle nuances of living life fully. I learned this from the human and other than human world as I made my way through the cities and countries of Great Britain, Europe, Africa and Israel. Unfortunately, I also lost this knowing for many years.

CHAPTER SIX

Returning

Finally on my way to yes
I bump into
all the places
where I said no
to my life
all the untended wounds
the red and purple scars
those hieroglyphs of pain
carved into my skin, my bones,
those coded messages
that send me down
the wrong street
again and again
where I find them
the old wounds
the old misdirection's
and I lift them
one by one
close to my heart
and I say
Holy Holy.

Persha Gertler

I was craving everything American: the smell of bacon and eggs on a lazy Sunday morning, the ability to hop in the car and run uptown for a carton of milk, the music and ceremony of patriotic parades that had moved me to tears, people of diverse backgrounds in one small area and the needle top of the Washington Monument separating the clear blue sky. It was time to come home.

Whenever someone asked about my trip, I struggled to find the right way to communicate. The immensity of the experience felt good living inside me and I was happy to keep it there until I had time to sort it out, incorporate it into my life and ultimately give it voice. That took many years.

Too quickly, I had to face the reality of being twenty-five with no job, no money, no plans and no prospects. I was also dealing with substantial culture shock. Everything was so big and bright, particularly the grocery store. Big as a city block with aisles and aisles of food and fluorescent lighting, grocery shopping made me feel that I needed a pair of sunglasses and skis. The markets in Bavaria were small and quaint and when you came in and when you left, you were greeted by the words 'Gruss Got,' or God's greetings. I loved the sweetness of that. However, I was back in the swing of things in America in no time.

During my travels, I had missed my best friend's wedding and as my wedding gift to her, I promised I would come directly to her when I returned. So I bought a car and moved to Houston. Everything in Houston was larger than life: the quart size glasses of iced tea, the mammoth livestock, freeways, sunsets, smiles, cowboy boots, ten gallon hats, tight starched jeans and heat - the unbearable heat. I realized then that I didn't need to leave the country to experience culture shock, just needed to move to the Lone Star State. But I loved everything about it (except for the heat).

Houston in the 70's was an incredibly friendly town. It is often said that people in the south are friendlier than the north and I wondered if the weather had something to do with that - if the warm weather gave birth to warm people. After all, in the North we hibernate for half the year and when it is time to come out and play as the thaw comes around again, it takes awhile to remember how to be friendly and warm. This re-emerging time doesn't exist in the south. The people in Houston were open and warm and I found myself becoming equally outgoing and friendly. I found a job and became an eager student of Eastern religion and philosophy, which, at the time, was still relatively new to the West. I discovered yoga, chanting, meditation and spiritual awakening. I particularly resonated with the teachings of the Buddha: loving kindness, compassion and rightful living. According to the Buddha's teachings, humankind wishes only to avoid suffering and to be happy. He saw that desire is the cause of suffering and that the mind has the capacity to change our desires and, in turn, our suffering. His eightfold path is a means to accomplish this: right understanding, right thought, right speech, right action, right livelihood, right effort, right concentration and right mindfulness. It only sounds simple, yet it made sense to me. I also loved the richness of the Buddhist ceremony with the exotic scents of incense and herbs and the haunting sounds of the tambora and harmonium. Paradoxically, these are the same things I loved about Catholic Mass – incense, music, and chanting. It was a wonderful time of growth and exploration and I was enjoying the process of filling the empty spaces in me.

Every summer I left the oppressive heat of Houston and flew to Lake Placid to visit my dear friend, Patty who had been my friend at the International School in Taiwan. The lush foliage, inviting mountains, and cold mountain lakes called to me. I was also drawn to the exciting nightlife. People typically let loose when they are on vacation and the bars were full to capacity with wealthy tourists having a good time and blue-collar townies who resented them. Mostly, it was uneventful and I had a lot of fun. I spent my days alone, hiking in the mountains and my nights enjoying and observing life in the bars.

In the summer of 1978, on the plane back to Houston from Lake Placed, I sat next to the man who became my husband. I was completely engrossed in *The Thorn Birds* and this guy next to me wouldn't stop chatting about fishing with his niece Meredith. I pulled the book closer and closer to my face and mumbled "un huh" and "un uh" hoping that he would lose interest and let me read my book, but he persisted. Only later would I realize that this was totally out of character for the man I married – he is, by nature, shy and reserved.

But persist he did on that plane ride from Albany, New York to Houston, Texas. I also acted completely out of character when I gave him my phone number. I knew John would call and I knew I wouldn't go out with him but that is not what happened: he did call and we did go out.

No two people could be more different but when John held my hand, a deep feeling of comfort and ease came over me and I knew that I had come home. We were married November 24, 1979. I postponed that wedding three times until John gave me an ultimatum," one more time and it is off altogether."

The idea of "marriage" had me tied up in knots. I wondered: when "two become one," what happens to me? And what about "till death do we part?" How could anyone ever say that with full confidence? (I was relieved when our very progressive priest consented to leave that part out). What would happen to my tendency to run when things got too intense – where would I go? But mostly, I didn't want to become my mother – cooking, cleaning, washing, sewing, schlepping, and doing for everyone. It all looked like hard work and no fun. Would I find a balance? And, I wasn't sure I wanted to have children. Marriage as an institution seemed painfully one-side and the divorce rate spoke volumes. Even though I had this bone-chilling fear of getting married, I knew I loved this man; I knew he was the right man for me and I was unwilling to live without him. John heard my fears and concerns and we came to an agreement: he would do his own laundry, we would eat our meals out and we would hire someone to do the cleaning.

Over the years, I have wondered where my dread of marriage originated. It wasn't from my husband, who was incredibly low maintenance; he was as happy with a bowl of cheerios as with beef Wellington for dinner, and he was always supportive of my various endeavors and adventures. While I didn't want to become my mother, it was not because she wasn't happy with her life, and it wasn't because I was a product of an unhappy marriage. As I dug deeper for the source of my negative ideas about marriage, I remembered a class I took in undergraduate school called, "Marriage and the Family" and one lecture and class discussion particular focused on differences between a "vital marriage vs. non-vital marriage." The bulk of American marriages fell in the "non-vital" category which meant living as a couple, joyless and stuck. In vital marriages, partners shared love and life, sex, child rearing, hobbies, interests, and companionship. I remember discussing that, while most marriages start out vital, in reality, few stay that way and that it is unrealistic to expect anything more. I remember leaving that class disillusioned and despondent and later trying to discuss these ideas with my two female roommates who weren't nearly as interested in the topic as I was. I was painfully impressionable and I determined then, that I simply would never marry because I couldn't settle for a loveless, unhappy marriage. I imagine that those feelings, coupled with my deep fear of disappearing inside the "married couple" contributed to my dread of marriage. My fears of disappearing were based on hidden, confused memories from my childhood. I had only one point of reference for a man's love for me and that was my father. I don't ever remember his love being particularly forthcoming like my mother's love but I never doubted it. Yet, I was still struggling to be seen, to be visible, and I brought these old wounds into my relationship with this young man who wished only to love me and marry me.

Years later, I came to understand my fear of intimacy, but at the time I was torn apart. I found myself at my internist's office with a bleeding ulcer and his advice to me was simply, "get married." When he left the room, I dropped my head into my hands and wept. For him, the diagnosis and treatment was so simple, but for me, it was much more complicated and I didn't know why. A few seconds later, my doctor poked his head into the treatment room and said, "Stop obsessing Jacqui; just get married and everything else will work out." I took his advice and he was right.

I have come to know that these inexplicable fears that pop up in our lives typically have their origin in childhood. We usually have no recollection of the moment these feelings of sadness, anger or fear were set in motion so we nudge ourselves to get over it and move on. I did this until I reached thirty-seven, and then I decided I could suffer or I could dig a little deeper. I did dig deeper and I thought that was deep enough. But here I am, years later, looking for that wrong turn.

That doctor was right; marriage was working out well. Our honeymoon years were happy and busy: I went back to school to become a chiropractic physician which involved a five year commitment to coursework and an internship and John established a thriving architectural practice. My focus was narrow and extremely fulfilling: John and school.

CHAPTER SEVEN

Winds of Chaos

In the very middle of the chest, deep deep inside
Something has broken
And it hurts almost all the time.
Sometimes it gives birth to anxiety, fear, and panic.
Sometimes it gives birth to anger, resentment and blame.
Sometimes it gives birth to tears.
This is our kinship with all who have loved truly –
From beginningless time.
You, my dear friend, understand it well
This genuine heart of sadness can teach us great compassion.
It humbles The Arrogant and softens The Unkind
This genuine heart of sadness can teach us great
Fearlessness.
It awakens Those who prefer to sleep and pierces through
Indifference.
This continual ache of the human heart –
Broken by the Loss of all that we hold dear
Is this not a blessing
Which when accepted fully — can be shared
With all?

Ani Pema Chodron

In November, 1982, I had planned to meet my dear friend Sissy for breakfast at the Four Seasons in downtown Houston. She was in law school and I was in medical school, so we rarely had time to get together. Because it was Veteran's day and neither of us had class, we decided to meet for a decadent, calorie laden breakfast of omelets, raisin bread French toast spread with sweet raisin and walnut cream cheese, French roast coffee, and the most delicious home fries I've ever tasted. To prepare for the decadence, I had already run five miles and swam 45 minutes before our designated time of 9 a.m.

We never had our breakfast. I was abducted at gunpoint in the parking lot across from the Four Seasons during the busy downtown rush hour. As I was getting out of my car, my captor forced me back into my car, blind folded me, shoved me onto the crammed floor space on the passenger side of the front seat and drove away in my dark brown New Yorker.

I am, by nature, a fighter, so I jumped into the back seat to try and escape but he locked the doors from the front seat. I beat the windows with my feet, kicking and screaming, biting his hands and shoving him away. This only served to make him more angry and determined. He began strangling me until I had no more fight and no more breath and I momentarily slipped away. All I could think of was my husband not knowing where I was, waiting patiently for me to come home, and then becoming a widower at such a young age. I did the only thing I could, I prayed. He forced me back onto the floor of the passenger side front seat and started beating me on the head so that I wouldn't try to escape again. I started talking to this man to try to calm him down, to calm me down, asking him questions about his life. This gave me time to think about what to do next.

I listened intently to the sounds around me to figure out where I was going; I listened for railroad tracks, construction sounds, the noisy traffic of freeways and sirens, but nothing rang familiar. His destination was a big open field where he stopped the car and asked for my money and jewelry. He was agitated and impatient and couldn't be bothered to wait so he ripped it off: gold necklaces, bracelets, diamond ring, pinky ring and $40.00. It was hardly worth the effort.

Hope was seeping into me and I began thinking that this was simply a robbery and that he would take the money and leave to get high. I prayed for this to happen, I prayed for my life and I prayed that I would have the strength to do whatever I needed to do next because my fight or flight adrenaline rush had given way to pure exhaustion and fear.

It seemed like minutes passed, but I'm sure it was only seconds. I tried to become smaller and smaller, to disappear into the floor mat and become part of the invisible joining of grass, gasoline, dirt and food crumbs that was ground into the mat that was pressed against my face. But he had other plans. He reached for me and pulled me off the floor towards him. I received that burst of energy that I had prayed for and became a crazy woman, hitting and kicking, biting and screaming, fighting with all my might so that when he tried to rape me he was unable to perform. All these years later, I remember his exact words, "I was going to rape you bitch but you are such a feisty bitch, I lost my mood."

I was thankful that he lost his mood. I was exhausted, I had fractured ribs, whiplash from the strangling and lacerations from head to toe from the ripping off of the jewelry and the fighting, but I was beginning to think I was going to live. He began brandishing what appeared to be a gun in front of my face again, but it probably wasn't a real gun, it was always hidden behind his jacket. He told me to stay on the floor for ten minutes while he got away and if I got up he would kill me. I waited what seemed like an eternity and slowly lifted my head up to peek out. I could still see him running, so I slid back down for another minute and then got out of the car, grabbed the keys which he'd left on the roof of the car, got back inside and locked all the doors and windows. All my fear and exhaustion gave way to deep, raw emotion and I wept like a frightened child who doesn't understand why she is being punished. Although the therapists I saw afterward called it rape, technically, it wasn't. The police identified it as an abduction and sexual molestation but I felt raped in every sense of the word; everything had been ripped away from me: innocence, trust, safety and faith in goodness.

I longed to be home; to be safe and comforted but I didn't know how to get home. I started the car and drove around the field until I found a way out. Then I drove straight to the closest gas station to use the payphone to call John. I avoided all eye contact with the attendants there because I was brimming with raw emotion. In his calm and steady voice, John assured me I was fine now, I just needed to get home, take a nice long shower and wash it away. Then he asked me some simple questions like: Can you see the Houston downtown skyline, the Pennzoil Building? Are there any cranes in the air working on new buildings (as an architect, he knew every building under construction in the downtown area)? Can you see the freeway from where you are? We went on like this until we figured out where I was and he directed me home. The police came later that day to take my report and I tried to move forward but I had lost my faith that I would ever be safe again.

Men don't rape because they love sex, anymore than alcoholics drink because they are thirsty. It's about fear and anger, hate and abuse, powerlessness and control; and it is rarely about the victim. It took me years to understand this. Sometimes, awful experiences leave a crack in our soul which allows God to slip in and direct us. And sometimes, these horrible incidents bring us to our knees and it is here, on our knees, that we hear the voice of God.

Up to that moment, I believed every cloud had a silver lining, but I could not find that silver lining. I was changed. Nothing made sense anymore. I asked myself over and over what was wrong, how could I make it better, what would make me feel whole again? I couldn't access my old strength. I felt as though my insides had been ripped out and left, raw and bloody, on the filthy floor of the car; my core was empty and my heart was completely broken.

I told myself to relax and stop crying, that it was all over, that these things don't happen twice. I told myself to surrender my fear. I told myself that people are raped every day and that they go on with their lives. It was time to pull myself together. I hired and fired a number of therapists, none of who helped me feel better or safer. I was trying, I really was, but I wasn't making any progress.

My dear friend Joe tried to convince me that this rape had burned up any and all bad karma in my life and that it would be smooth sailing from here on out. I needed to believe him. I needed to believe something.

John's family was coming to Houston for Thanksgiving just after this trauma. We planned for the men to attend a basketball game and the women to go downtown to see a show. The problem was that I would be the one to drive and park in the underground parking. I was terrified and I obsessed about this for weeks. Finally, my in-laws arrived but I was unable to speak of my fear or of my abduction, so I prayed all the way to the theater. I thought about my bad karma being burnt up as I got out of the car and walked to the elevator. I don't remember the show because all I thought about was walking back to the underground parking in the dark to come home. For two years I hitchhiked through Europe with only a pack on my back, yet I couldn't cross a parking lot at home in Houston. I had never known how crippling fear can be.

All aspects of my life were affected. Shopping was impossible unless it was during the day and I was able to find a parking space directly in front of the entrance. I once drove to a Doctor's appointment but I was too frightened to park in the parking garage. Fiercely independent, I became frightened and pathetic. Houston became a very scary place.

I started taking a self-defense class but I was unable to continue because I was too physically broken. I told myself if I had taken karate instead of yoga I might have been able to protect myself. But nothing would have altered the outcome. I couldn't stop trying to make sense of it. And while it completely broke me, many years later, I realized it broke me open to a greater understanding of the pain and suffering of the world: our collective suffering. I believe this is a lesson that I was meant to learn. For me, this learning has come in waves; I have been piecing this puzzle together for many years.

I believe that, along with our own biochemical individuality, we have our own spiritual template and we learn and grow based on that template. It doesn't matter how we come to truth, or how long it takes, it just matters that we are on our way. For me, this journey has taken years but for others it can come with one big bang. When I am having one of my spiritual temper tantrums and behaving like a spoiled brat during a rather lopsided fight with God, I find myself envious of this timing. But mostly I am happy to be on this journey in whatever shape it takes.

We all experience angst and sadness, pain and suffering and feelings of inadequacy. We all long for something deeply meaningful, peaceful and fulfilling. We long for the Divine. We long to ride the sweet gentle tide of Oneness. Yet, many of us don't know what that means; never mind how to get there. I don't pretend to have answers. I just know that when I take the biblical quote from Matthew literally, "Ask and you shall receive," I ask - I ask constantly - and I receive.

Healing doesn't happen just because we want it to and we think it is time. I believe we must figure out what sapped the life out of us and why. I've been compelled to ferret out how the trauma of being raped may have amplified other past traumas which together completely annihilated my essence. While the rape clearly "broke the camel's back," I needed to know what had weakened me to the point where I broke so easily. I felt I had no choice but to pursue this inquiry because I was dying inside and I wanted to live again. The process of inquiry at that time is similar to my recent search for the wrong turn: both are a search into the emotional, physical and spiritual body to find what is creating the void or disconnect; followed by a sincere effort to make it right again – to heal. I am constantly doing this in my life – shaping and re-shaping. It is much like creating a sculpture. The sculptor throws a little clay, shapes it, throws more, shapes it again, takes some off, and molds the old to the new, continually shaping and re-shaping. When the process is complete, the piece of work stands tall and firm, rigid and yet soft, a thing of beauty. This is how we shape and re-shape ourselves with every opportunity that comes. Creating our lives doesn't happen overnight. It is a long process - and love and forgiveness are usually at the heart of it; not just forgiving others, but loving and forgiving ourselves.

After the rape, John was a great comfort to me. He let me know I was safe: he held me while I cried and chauffeured me around when I was feeling vulnerable. He even accompanied me Christmas shopping (the one thing he hates the most!). All this went a long way towards healing and soon I was pregnant.

On August 18, 1983 as Hurricane Alicia was making her way toward the coast of Texas, my first born chose to arrive. All the preparations had been made for a home birth. My husband and I had taken Bradley Method Childbirth classes preparing for a home birth with the assistance of a nurse midwife. My family and friends were not supportive and we fielded many of their phone calls imploring us to reconsider our decision. I realize this was out of love and concern for me and my child but I was getting testy by the fourth month when the phone calls stopped.

Our pediatrician assured us home births were safe and said he would come to our home as soon as the baby arrived. My philosophy is that hospitals are for sick people and I was pregnant, not sick. I wanted to relax and give birth in the privacy of my own home. We took care of the paperwork at the hospital weeks in advance in the event that I needed to be transported there and we had made many trips to the hospital to determine the best route and the shortest time. We were definitely ready for this birth; however, we had not counted on Hurricane Alicia.

The midwives called the mothers who were due the week before and after Alicia was scheduled to hit, to warn of the increased probability that the drop in barometric pressure during a hurricane could cause us to go into labor prematurely. They invited all of us to come to the birthing center the day prior to the hurricane and stay there until it passed. This way, the midwives would be able to tend to whoever went into labor. That sounded awful to me and I decided to take my chances at home. We went to the birthing center to pick up the cord clamp and a few odds and ends that we would need for the birth and we settled in.

Alicia came barreling in with deafening wind gusts and tornados and blinding fury. The rain pelted eerily against the windows and the sides of the house. The trees were twisting and bowing in grotesque and unnatural positions. Twigs, branches, leaves, trash cans, patio furniture, rakes and shovels flew through the air. My fear was building to such a crescendo that I couldn't tell if it was my insides roaring or the wind. So I prayed. I sat on the floor under the kitchen table, which seemed like the safest spot in the house, and I prayed for the safety of my unborn child.

As day turned to night, we decided to go to bed and try and get some rest because there would be unimaginable clean up in the morning. As we lay in bed, my husband talking softly to try and calm my nerves, my mind wandered outside our bedroom window to the enormous oak tree swaying back and forth. I asked John what the chances were of that beautiful tree uprooting and falling into the house. He explained calmly and certainly, as one might talk to a child, that this was a 150-year-old tree, that it was anchored deeply and securely and that it had withstood far more in his long life than this hurricane. So, I took a deep breath, relaxed, thanked him for being so kind to me, closed my eyes for an instant and then bolted upright when a thunderous crack shook me to the core. "Oh my God, what was that?" I screamed. John answered simply, "The oak tree. It's in our living room." Then imagining the tree was on fire, I started yelling, "Oh my God, the tree is on fire, and our house will burn down!" In actuality, the shooting flames were coming from outside the window; it was our two transformer boxes that had burst into flames because they, too, had been hit by lightning.

My husband was trying to keep me calm but I was in a full throttle panic. I kept rubbing my tummy and saying to the baby, "Just relax, everything is fine, please don't come now because we have no electricity, no running water and I know you would much rather be born at home than the hospital." I repeated this mantra as I resumed my spot underneath the kitchen table while John braved the storm to check on things outside. What the midwives had said about the effects of dropping barometric pressure on labor kept running through my mind as I prayed for my child to please wait. Then I made a pact with God. "If you let us live, and promise no more trees will fall through the roof, and make the electricity come on before this precious baby bursts into our lives, I promise to be the best mother ever." And so it was: Kieran Thomas Martin was born at home six days later, shortly after the electricity returned. The pact was sealed and my work was cut out for me. Of course, I realize that God doesn't make deals, but I had asked, and, it seemed something answered. So, with deep gratitude, I honored my side of the bargain.

We still laugh about that old oak tree. I knew in my bones that tree was coming down; I just wanted someone to tell me it wasn't. Up to that point in our relationship, I believed what John told me unequivocally, but not after that. It wasn't that I no longer believed anything he said, it was that I stopped asking all those inane questions like, "Do you think it will rain today?" or "Do you suppose Carter will win the election?" or "Do you suppose that tree will come down?" I realized I knew the answers to my own questions as well as or better than he did. We still joke about John falling from grace that night, but it wasn't like that, I just trusted more in my knowing.

Morning finally arrived and all the earthly elements had quieted: the raging winds and pelting rain had stopped, the tornados ran out of steam and the sun was shining as if to say, "See, everything always settles down and I always follow." The oak tree had split: half was in our living room and the other half, the larger half, lay across our driveway. In the event that I needed to be transported to the hospital due to complications with the birth that felled tree would make transport impossible. Therefore, it had to be moved immediately. Thankfully, we lived in a wonderful neighborhood where everyone helped each other out.

The neighbors began arriving from up and down the street, bearing chain saws, ropes and shovels. The neighborhood was in shambles, trees and debris were everywhere and it seemed we were facing an overwhelming task. Our home was first because of "that enormous pregnant women with the tree blocking her drive." It took many men, many chainsaws and many hours to cut and remove that tree and I was delighted and relieved when it was accomplished. Since most of the city had no electricity, we packed our bags and followed the electricity: we stayed two nights with one set of friends and two night with others until our electricity came back on. I knew my condition was making my friends nervous and uncomfortable because my home birth would be in their home if this baby decided to come. Luckily, that didn't happen.

We arrived home the day our electricity was restored and we prepared for the birth of our child. Our baby was conceived a month following my rape and as I prepared for the birth, I wondered, as I had so many times over the past nine months, what effect my sadness and heartbreak stemming from it, might have on my unborn child. Literature suggests that the fetus is aware as it is growing and that the soul slips in and out of the fetus during his or her development; staying more permanently towards the last month or two. I tried to accept the blessing of new life as a positive exchange for the sadness and pain that had preceded it. I had talked to my baby in utero much of each day, always in an upbeat voice and with love in my heart. I prayed to the giver of this gift to prevent any negativity from seeping through to this precious unborn child. That's all I could do.

It is amazing to me how our mind and will can control our body and make it wait for something as important as a birth. Our pediatrician determined that our baby boy was two or three days late based on the dry peeling skin on the soles of his feet and the palms of his hands. In every other way, he was unbelievably perfect and so was the delivery. Labor was just that, a labor of love: I swam, walked, squatted, sat on the toilet, received chiropractic adjustments and acupuncture and did a lot of breathing while I waited patiently for Kieran to arrive. John cut the cord and our baby boy followed his dad with his eyes all around the room. It was magical. Sacred. I was stitched and took the baby to my breast. Gazing into his eyes, I realized that I was spiritually ill-prepared for him. So, I quickly added a short addendum to my previous agreement with the Divine, "And please keep me one huge spiritual step ahead of him until he is grown." In retrospect, that simple statement placed me on an entirely new path, a path that wasn't always comfortable because so much of my life changed: friends, interests, philosophy, diet, religion, and spiritual leanings and beliefs. My heart was opening, big and wide.

Although humans and animals have been giving birth since time immemorial, I believed that birthing my child was the most sacred and unique experience of all time, like all mothers will tell you.

Ten months earlier, a man holding a whirlwind of anger, drug induced aggression and frustration brought immense personal devastation to me. Later, Hurricane Alicia blew through Houston bringing with it unbelievable devastation to the entire Southeast coast. Both of these winds blew tremendous chaos into our lives but the morning my son was born, I saw hope and love in his face; I saw the face of the Divine shining back at me and I knew that everything was as it should be.

CHAPTER EIGHT

Generations of pain

It is possible I am pushing through solid rock
in flint like layers, as the ore lies, alone;
I am such a long way in I see no way through,
and no space: everything is close to my face,
and everything close to my face is stone.
I don't have much knowledge yet in grief –
so this massive darkness makes me feel small.
YOU be the master: make yourself fierce, break in:
then your great transforming will happen to me,
and my great grief cry will happen to you.

Rilke

Mothering is very simple and pure because all an infant needs is love and nourishment. It is a perfect set-up because the babies need for sustenance encourages the mother to be completely present and engaged. This builds a beautiful bond almost instantaneously between mother and child. When a mother takes her child to her breast, she becomes the universal, archetypical mother – the source and the giver. Embodying this mother energy, I felt one with all the mothers of the ages. I felt humbled and blessed to be a part of this lineage of generations of powerful women who have perpetuated life: offering love, nourishment, protection, guidance and ultimately freedom. I suddenly realized that there would be no other job for me that would be as important.

I never dreamt that I could be completely entertained by a baby for hours; a baby who just lay there, passed gas, ate occasionally, smiled and slept. We were completely mesmerized by our child and we wondered what we had ever done before to fill up our time.

It is often a tremendous struggle for moms to go back to work after the birth of a child, especially a first-born. Many of us want it all and also know that if we give up our lives for our children, we run the risk of ending up depressed, dissatisfied and resentful. So, as my six-week break from school came to an end, I bundled up my son and took him to school with me. While I was in class, he stayed with a friend's wife who had young children at home. This arrangement worked well for the time that I was nursing. I was lucky; I had marvelous support and a very easy and content child. John shared in all the responsibilities of child rearing including regularly taking Kieran to his office. Also, our neighbor Liz, a quintessential mother, kept Kieran for us. There is immense truth in the old adage that if Mom is happy, everyone is happy. And everyone was happy.

Over the next eighteen months, I finished school, completed my internship, took my boards and set up practice. Two months later, twenty months after her brother, our beautiful daughter, Meghan Marie Martin was born. She was also born at home in Houston but without the fanfare of a major hurricane. Nevertheless, she was her own little storm, all ten pounds, two ounces of her.

I continue to be fascinated by how two children can be so different. They both share the exact same gene pool and yet they came into this world with their own little personalities. Kieran was an easy child from the start. While he was intense, he was also sweet, gentle and easy going. Meghan entered the world kicking and screaming. She is aware, determined, demanding and intensely loyal. I love these differences. Over the years, I've come to believe that genes are not the only factor in play when our children enter our lives. I see how both the parents' and the children's soul needs play an important part in how we come together. It seems that new souls come into this world not only to learn from their parents but also to teach them. When my daughter was young and peeved with me, I would often tell her," Look, sweetie, you chose me to be your mom, so get over it." And she would fire back, "There is no way I would have chosen you to be my mom." And then I would just smile and say that I was thrilled with the choices we had made.

As new mothers can attest to, life is intense with newborns until you find your rhythm. I observed other women to see how they managed with a blossoming new family. We all do it differently and we do it according to who we are at the time. Some women are born to mother; they make everything look easy. Others, like me, struggle. Some give in to the chaos. Others pop in and out and defer to a nanny for the fundamental care giving like getting the children dressed, fed, and to school. Yet, no matter what our style and preferences, we all try to find a balance. We try not to resent our husbands for not enjoying midnight feedings and for not being completely present when there are other, seemingly more important, things to be done like work. We try, when we are at home, to be present and make that time count. We work it out. I became controlling which worked at the time but later came back to haunt me. I needed to know that everything was in order: that patients were doing the protocol I set up; I wanted to know where the children were at any given time; I didn't want the T.V. on, ever; I wanted only healthy food to go into my family's mouths – I was insufferable. I know better than to think that I am in control of anything and everything that is happening in my life but that is how I learned to get through the intense times. More recently, I have learned to relax my grip but there is still plenty of room for improvement.

Following Meghan's birth, we hired a nanny, Tuong, who simplified my life and became deeply bonded with Meghan. They shared that rare kind of heart connection we feel with certain people upon meeting them, as though we have known them all our lives. I felt immensely blessed by the gift of support for my children. Some nights when Tuong would go home, she would predict that Meghan would get sick during the night with a slight fever, but that by morning she would be fine. And it happened just like that. She told me that Vietnamese mothers sleep with their children until they are two, perhaps honing their intuition about their children. And she seemed to know what they needed to eat when they didn't feel well (Vietnamese foods that I knew nothing about) and to anticipate when they needed to pee or poop. Her knowing alleviated our anxiety over everything, including potty training. Tuong's calm balanced my angst and our lives glided gracefully along.

I discerned how my children were doing by looking into their eyes. I especially loved seeing life through their eyes when they were excited about a new discovery. But when I saw vacancy in the eyes of my children, it took my breath away. My son's eyes went vacant the year he attended a beautiful, highly acclaimed preschool. When my husband and I arrived for his first parent-teacher meeting, we were shown a poster on his desk full of pictures of Kieran performing various activities during his first six weeks at school. I looked hard at each pictures and I was disturbed by the blank look in those precious eyes: he had checked out. I began asking the teacher simple questions: does Kieran seem to be enjoying himself? Who does he play with? What subjects interest him most? Does he laugh much? I realized that she had no clue about my child. She knew nothing about this gentle soul who had been sitting in her classroom every day for the last six weeks. So I pulled him out and moved him to the school that my daughter attended: – Trinity School for Young Children where every day was sweet and fun. I asked myself what I was thinking to put my sweet, soulful child in a school where pre-kindergarteners wore uniforms, took two languages (Spanish and Greek) and sat in rows of hard wooden desks. In retrospect, I had chosen this preschool because it had been highly recommended and, having interviewed six other schools, found it to be the strongest in overall curriculum. But who needs "strong" at that age when every day should be a love fest; loose, unregimented and supportive.

Meghan and Kieran were happy at Trinity School and they were having fun, which is exactly what preschoolers are meant to do. Once a week, the otherwise pristine playground was transformed into a warm mushy mess of mud. Thursday was "Mud Puddle Pig" day. Children arrived at school with a change of clothes and were encouraged to wallow in the mud, just like a pig! A hose ran water down the small sliding board allowing for a smooth sail into the marvelous muddy puddle below. This was pure heaven for the children whose giggles and squeals could be heard from a block away.

I now understand the allure of mud. Many years later, on a trip to Costa Rica, my friend Judy and I leased a couple of horses and a guide and rode far into the mountains to a hot spring and a mud bath. How wonderful to rub the soft, cool, oozing chocolate brown mud all over my body and then submerge myself in that bubbly hot water. It was like heaven on earth. Even now, I have to smile remembering how it felt like Mother Earth wrapping her warm, dark arms around me in a calm and reassuring hug. That's connection: true, primal connection. I learned then that the comfort, the knowing, and the sense of belonging that comes from connecting deeply with the earth, has everything to do with being healthy of body, mind, and spirit. I did not see that connection in my son's eyes at his first preschool; but his entire body screamed it when he was playing in the mud at his new school. He was happier and, as a result of that, healthier. He felt "connected."

Of course children don't come into this world with an instruction manual hanging from their tiny wrists, as I often wished, but they do let us know, sometimes subtly, how to care for them and for ourselves. They let us see through their eyes how our lives look. They are, in many ways, our greatest teachers when we are open to the lessons. My children have taught me much more than I have taught them. And they have taught me, through their eyes and body posture, how to help them when they are unable and/or unwilling to speak their needs. It was through my own eyes, looking back at me through my daughter's eyes, that I found my deepest hidden and most revealing story.

I had just bathed Meghan and I was singing to her as I dried her off. John came into the bedroom to chat. Scowling at him and through gritted teeth, I hissed, "If you ever touch her, I'll kill you with my bare hands. I mean it." Incredulous, he looked at me and said softly as he turned white with fear and concern, "I have no idea what you're talking about, Jacqui, but you're scaring me and I'm going to turn around and leave. I'll be at the office if you need me." In that second, I had become someone else. I didn't know what I was talking about either but I did know this was not about

Meghan or her father. Suddenly, I was conscious of a deep, painful wound that I had been hiding from myself so that I could function as a normal person. Maintaining that facade may have served me once, but waking up to the truth meant that now the fragile, glass house that I had built for myself was beginning to shatter, revealing a lucid memory of sexual impropriety. The searing rage that erupted towards my husband, was actually the misplaced, pent-up rage I felt toward my father. At age thirty-six, I found the courage and motivation to begin to uncover and bring forward, in the best way I could at the time, this shadow aspect of my experience that had been hovering in the darkness for years and now was nipping at my heels. Nobody can dictate when the time is right to shine the light of attention on the dark corners of the psyche, although many people had tried. The power of my early childhood memory surfacing shook my entire being; it was my first realization of how our lives are mirrored back to us through our children, particularly mothers and their daughters and fathers and their sons. I knew that this was a momentous re-living of a buried memory and I knew it was time to face it.

Since my junior year in college, I had been seeking counsel from various people in the healing profession for my persistent and nagging feeling that something wasn't right in my life. I sensed there was something dark and ugly hiding inside me. I had been told for years by therapists, healers, re-birthers, shaman, clairvoyants and hypnotists that I had all the signs of having been sexually abused, and my response was always the same: "You obviously have me confused with someone else." Then I proceeded to fire each one of them. It seems silly now, looking back, to have sought help from renowned healers and then refused to be open to what they had to say. But after that devastating experience with Meghan, John and I, I eventually recognized that I could no longer sustain my denial.

I don't pretend to be able to access exactly what I was thinking or feeling when I was three, or six or seven. But I imagine I wanted to please my parents and to be loved like all children. Hundreds of books have been written on the subject of abuse and I am sure they are very helpful but I have chosen not to read them. I have this notion that if I bring something close and give it a name, particularly a name held by the collective or general population, then I will receive the energy that comes along with that. I didn't want anything that I read to interfere with my own personal journey of healing. And I didn't want the collective energy of abuse to become mine. I think that each of us ultimately comes to our own way of healing. My way has always been to turn to the spiritual world for help. So, I started by begging and pleaded with God to erase this raw pain from my heart and let me move on. And then I waited, and waited, and then waited some more.

Maneuvering through sexual abuse has been my most difficult journey. I take five steps forward and then two back. In reflection, I see periods in which my life has unfolded smoothly and I experience moving forward with clear purpose and an open and forgiving heart. Then in one moment, something de-rails me and I find myself back where I started, angry, sad and hurt. This looping has confounded me and I have grown weary of the struggle and yet I know that forgiving and loving again is a process not an event. It takes time, patience, and courage.

The complexity of the human psyche with its resilience and brilliant filing system is remarkable to me. For close to forty years my mind had been shuffling memories further and further back into the recesses of my mind so that these memories couldn't hurt me. On those rare occasions when those memories came forward, I would get depressed and shove them back and somehow "forget" again, thus restoring a certain kind of peace and order. This is how denial works; it's a marvelous check and balance system for coping with trauma. I believe my rape and abduction in Houston loosened the memory of childhood abuse and allowed it to surface so I could look at it if I chose to. We are largely aware of what we can and can't handle emotionally, physically and spiritually and when there are doubts, the unconscious helps out. My psyche wanted to forget these memories even though therapists and other healers, as well as my own memories, dreams, and meditations had repeatedly raised the question of past sexual abuse. I simply wasn't opening. Later, when the time was right, I began my process of opening to the truth of my experience.

At first, I seemed to be walking many parallel roads: one soft and spiritual, another more human and edgy. Still another path meant walking hand in hand with denial and one involved shoving all that darkness back behind the door that I had recently agreed to open. I imagine that this was my psyche's way of protecting me from too much hurt, this constant flitting from one coping style to the next, skimming the surface but never landing. These paths ultimately merged into one as I became stronger. For the first few years, I was unwilling to discuss this with anyone, including my husband. I quietly began a private, profound and painful process of acknowledging, forgiving and moving forward.

Initially, I stopped going to my family home. There was no shortage of reasons with a hectic life and two busy children. Once, my daughter asked me why we weren't in any of the family pictures. I told her we were only in some, but not all of them. When I did go home, I became wretchedly ill: vomiting, diarrhea and pure exhaustion. And it became a joke: "Jacqui always gets sick when she's around us." Like the way I reacted to visiting Dachau, purging seems to be my way of dealing with raw emotion and I am thankful to my body for taking over when my emotions and spirit simply can not.

Finally, I became furious with my father. Neither he, nor anyone else knows about this, but one day I woke up and I had hate in my heart. My heart was completely closed and I felt engulfed in a large dark field whenever I thought about him. Hatred is an awful emotion because the only person that suffers from it is the one filled with hate, which was me. I suppose Confucius was right when he said, "Before you embark on a journey of revenge, dig two graves."

I believe it was crucial for me to face my hatred for my father - that shadow side of me that wasn't "pretty" or "nice," but real and honest. Soon, I felt ready to forgive but forgiveness was illusive. I begged and cajoled, threw temper tantrums and threatened, but I couldn't forgive my father. In retrospect, I see there wasn't enough room in my heart for forgiveness because it was completely full of blame and anger. This was a difficult time for me because my hatred was destroying my heart. I felt empty-hearted and sad. I prayed a lot. I prayed to the gods of forgiveness and compassion to help me: I prayed to Jesus, who personifies forgiveness to me and to Avalokeshvara, the boddhitsava of compassion. I begged for their help. I did exercises and rituals and ceremony. I kept praying. I kept pleading. I kept asking.

Finally, my heart felt the sweet nectar of forgiveness seeping through. I struggled to open enough to see the bigger picture; the hideous entanglement of abuse. I do believe, in my purest heart, that my father loved me and meant no harm. He perpetuated a behavior that had tragic results; it was devastating, confusing and shrouded in secrecy. And it was the root of immense sadness for me over the course of my lifetime. I suppose someone - his father or mother- sexually abused him and their parents before them. This behavior is not personal, logical, or intended to harm. It is familial, lives in our cell tissue, and is passed down from one generation to the next. And so I visualized giving this pain and suffering back, from generation to generation, back to the beginning of time, back to God, who would purify and eliminate it. I imagined I was not the owner of these emotions and that it was time to let go of my pain and suffering. As my heart opened, I perceived the collective heartbreak of hundreds of generations, each person receiving pain and then doing the personal work of learning to let it go. This is not only my story; it is our collective story. This understanding was humbling and softening and heartbreaking but mostly it was healing. Seeing the bigger picture - the multi-generational story- made it easier to extricate myself from the victim archetype and step towards wholeness.

I have continued to explore the concept of "collective heartbreak" - the back story to my smaller story. It is a story that we all share, and this perspective helps us understand and have compassion, not only for our own pain but for others' as well. Suffering, then, can function as a vehicle for understanding and once we have experienced it, we can release it and help others do the same.

Every time we looked at a potential new home, John spent a lot of time in the basement. At first, I couldn't fathom his fascination with basements, but he explained that without a good foundation, the house would be a constant source of problems. He was looking for cracks and crevices - anything that would compromise the integrity of the building. This is how I have come to look at my body, soul and spirit - I routinely check the foundation. I think that childhood trauma can crack our foundation before it has had the time to grow strong enough to support us properly. Sometimes these cracks manifest in physical ailments like back pain or weakness, or lower abdominal problems and inertia. And in those times when I don't have the energy to move forward, I use a guided meditation to see if I can't identify those cracks and crevices and cement them with love so that I can feel whole again.

Ultimately, it was pure grace that softened my heart, extended her hand to me, and walked me across the threshold away from pain and toward understanding, forgiveness and, yes, gratitude. I am thankful for the softening of the wall I have built around me. I am thankful for the love and forgiveness I have given to myself and others and how that has nurtured my relationships. And, I am happy to have loosened my crusty edge and to become more approachable. I have relaxed into myself, and while I am not completely home, I have found comfort on the journey.

Years later, prior to a visit home to visit my dying mother, I sunk into blame and anger. I wanted so much to be able to offer my love and support to her and I knew I needed to get over myself and move into a gentler place. Instead of my old habit of pushing it away, I decided to bring my misery close and hold it gently as though it were a sacred blessing. So, I sat quietly, eyes closed, heart opened, holding misery as a precious gift and it became like a beautiful crystal bowl of shimmering blue diamonds. It was breathtaking. I believe misery is sacred. We must whisper before it because the Divine is present in our misery. In fact, in our deepest misery, when we are weak with sorrow and all fight has been wept out of us, God slips in. He holds us gently and sweetly and whispers in our ear that, yes, we can go on, that our heart is healing even now as we weep. I know this is true because I am able to come back, firmer and stronger and willing to love again after I have accepted misery.

Ultimately, I knew that I must make a choice: live crippled or dig deep and forgive. I believe that we have contracted to learn from particular incidents in our life and we will be given the opportunity again and again until we are ready to embrace the lesson. So, my notion of a wrong turn is ludicrous in the face of this. Childhood abuse is slimy and slick. Like an oil spill, it is extremely difficult to disentangle the debris and clean it up. In my innocence, I felt responsible, dirty, unworthy and unlovable. I accepted these emotions and went into hiding. I hid behind a great wall so I could be invisible, safe, and inaccessible and I lived in this place for many years. But I grew lonely and sad. When I chose to face my demons, I fell deeper into the mire of abuse because I had become comfortable living in denial. On the other side of the darkness, I found forgiveness in my protected heart, not only for me, but for the ones I love. This forgiveness has opened me to the richness in life: I feel freer, less defended, more engaged and more comfortable in my body. I still struggle and I still feel sadness but the journey is far more enjoyable.

We can't circumvent truth, or take a pass, or a shortcut to avoid that truth. We are given the chance to see life through clear eyes and we can come to this from any direction we like. Or we can re-visit it in another lifetime. It is our choice.

CHAPTER NINE

New Trails

*A man never arises so high
As when he knows not
Whither he is going.*

Oliver Cromwell

In the summer of 1989, we left Houston, our friends, and our businesses and moved to a small town in northwest Connecticut. I was tired of living in fear and constantly looking over my shoulder in the big city. We both wanted to be closer to family and I wanted to heal and feel safe again. John had been courted by a firm that he had worked for during his summers in Connecticut and I decided to take some time off from practicing as a chiropractic physician. Once the children returned to school that fall, however, I realized that I am much happier working, so I opened an office in the center of town.

As we started fresh with our careers, schools, support system, friends and affiliations, I began to relax and I knew we had made a good choice to move back east. It was easier for me because I had started over many times in my life. My husband is much slower to make friends and acquaintances but with time developed a small circle of friends. Our children, who were both under six years old, took about two seconds to get acquainted and fit in. We all found a nice, comfortable rhythm.

John was accustomed to small town living because he grew up in a small farming town in eastern Connecticut. When he was a child, the population of Scotland, Connecticut was 900 and it is still today. I was accustomed to cities and a healthy dose of anonymity, but anonymity is a small price to pay for feeling safe and supported.

One of my favorite memories of life in a small town was when the children were young and attended CCD (Confraternity of Christian Doctrine) classes. Wednesday was the day that all the Catholic children went to CCD. The priest would walk up to the school in his collar and robe to collect the six to nine year old CCD students and bring them back to the church for class. This was a four-block walk. The children followed him, pushing and shoving, laughing and giggling back up the street to the church as though he were the Pied Piper. I think many of the neighborhood children wished they were Catholic on Wednesdays because the CCD students seemed to be having such a good time. Some of those kids would walk along with them just to join in the fun. It always made me smile when I watched them pass by my office window. It was an idyllic and safe place to raise our children and because of that, we were thrilled with our decision to move east.

Professionally, I found Connecticut less open than Houston to complementary medicine. In fact, I felt I had taken a step back in time. This was difficult for me in the beginning but I learned to adjust my treatment techniques to accommodate the medically conservative climate of the area, even though I felt like I was clipping my healing wings. I deeply respect and honor science in my treatment of patients but what enables me to be particularly effective is my integration of science and intuition. I felt I had to minimize expressing my intuitive skills in order to fit in. I can't always explain how I know what I know. For example, when I send patients for tests to support my feelings, my hunch about their condition won't show up until years later. But if I couldn't immediately and definitively confirm my suspicions with tests that support it, then I appeared unprofessional or "flakey." So I found myself in a quandary. A colleague once asked me why I was leaving the best part of myself at home, the part of me that was deeply spiritual and intuitive, when I went to the office. I realize now that I wasn't strong enough then to be different.

Our lives were full and busy as our focus shifted from our professional lives to our children's activities: soccer games, basketball games, crew meets, girl scouts and boy scouts, class trips, Disney World, family trips, hiking and camping, birthday parties, and all that comes with those family building years from birth to college. I truly enjoyed my role as a mother and I was having fun along side my children. The largest part of me felt full and complete but around the edges, restlessness was lurking. This restlessness was familiar and I often felt it slinking around in the shadows, especially when I had fallen into a comfortable rhythm. I call this a "quickening," a prelude to a shift in our lives that is just beneath the surface. But a quickening is also inconvenient, and I've often chosen to bulldoze through it and stay the course. Restlessness, boredom, frustration, anxiety and indifference are subtle, and not so subtle, indicators that our lives need tweaking, but who wants to tweak when things seem perfect. We can ignore these things until their presence becomes like an elephant in the room and then there is no choice. So, when Kieran and Meghan were twelve and ten respectively, and I was in my forties, I did some work with a Shaman. A Shamanic healer is an individual who has the ability to act as an intermediary between the spirit and human world and to then use that ability to help others. The woman who helped me immeasurably, is a third generation Curandera, the Spanish equivalent of a Shaman. She uses spiritual energy to assist in healing. This is a gift often passed down through the generations and I felt honored to be the recipient of this gift.

Through this work, I found that shifts in energy served to unblock, and even tame, some of my childhood memories. I finally understood how all of those seemingly ill-matched pieces fit together: fear of marriage and intimacy, deep depression following my rape, pathological protection of my female child at age three, perfectionist, driven, introverted, it all began to add up. Periodically through our lives, certain incidents activate our past and nudge us to peel back the veil that shrouds our hurts. Though, sometimes deep investigation is just too much to bear. I always wished I could accept life as it is doled out, and more importantly, accept myself just as I am. I have had many friends and patients over the years who had no desire to change or work at improving. For them, there was no reason to open Pandora's box. I am deeply covetous of this way of being. I have tried, on and off through my life, to be one who lives in the moment and lets go of everything else and yet, that is not who I am. I am a seeker and that has taken me to great depths and soaring heights. My challenge has been to delve into the darkness and embrace what I find. I have not always been a success at this, and sometimes it takes years, and the journey is often bittersweet, but the challenge nourishes my soul and my rewards are boundless.

We all wish we could be like someone else at different times in our life because they wear their life with such grace. But another's life wouldn't fit us. It is our life that we must learn to live in the best way we can and to be happy with that.

Whoever knows what goes on emotionally inside of another person? I sometimes look at friends and acquaintances and think how blessed they are to have such a wonderful life. And then, in one nano-second, that can all change, like 9-11.

Over the years, many patients have asked me how I came to be so serene and peaceful. They wanted to know how to be like me. These remarks always made me smile. We don't know from the outside looking in, what kind of pain or hurt or trauma someone is holding inside. I have seen over the years so many physical manifestations of lives gone awry with rampant diseases and illnesses. I have especially seen this in women because, as women, we try to shoulder the world in our small, fragile bodies. We hold so much inside and present ourselves to the world as strong, capable, compassionate, accomplished and bright beings. And we are all of this. But we are also sensitive, giving, caretakers who sometimes get lost in the shuffle. In my experience as a physician, I have seen that women tend to hold deep emotions in different parts of their bodies. Men more often present with well-defined pain, like low back or neck pain, and don't make a strong connection to an emotional component. It appears to me that men and women process life, and the concomitant emotions of life, differently. I began looking at this with fresh eyes as I learned more about the chakras.

The East has brought to the West a system of looking at the body and the energy that flows cyclically in the body from the base of the spine to the crown of the head. These energy circles, called chakras, relate to physical and spiritual power centers in the body. There are seven chakras; they operate together and build subtly, one upon another. They are meaningful because they tell our story – our history, biology, psychology and physiology - through the lens of energy medicine. This brilliant approach to health is another tool to help inform and explain our physical ailments. There are specific physical, emotional and spiritual issues that can be traced to a corresponding chakra. Many acupuncturists, me included, believe that the acupuncture meridians emanate from these chakras or power centers. A brief explanation of the chakras helps to understand how our history deeply affects our physiology.

The first chakra is located at the base of the spine at the pubic symphysis. It is symbolic of safety and security in the physical world, relating mostly to that first year of life. It is the foundation upon which everything else is built. So, when children are loved, nourished, sheltered and welcomed into the world, they will have a strong foundation and generally few physical problems in the lower pelvis. If however, a child enters life unwanted, abandoned, traumatized or physically abused, she will often manifest physical imbalances of the first chakra such as problems in the legs, lower spine, pelvis and large intestine.

The second chakra, located between the pubis and the umbilicus, relates to sex, power, and money. Whenever a patient presents with financial worries, divorce or job loss, very often, their low back is problematic and their energy is low in the second chakra. People who have experienced sexual abuse of any kind present with second chakra issues. For example, women will present with problems such as fibroids, endometriosis, infertility, menstrual pain, vaginal problems and ovarian and uterine diseases such as cancer. Similarly, men who have been sexually abused present with sexual problems such as impotence, prostate issues and cancers. Other second chakra imbalances include lower bowel problems, constipation and bladder problems. Some of the more common emotional difficulties related to the second chakra are problems with sexual desire or performance, problems with relationships, issues of control, lack of self confidence particularly as it relates to finances, fear, and resentment.

When I incorporated what I'd learned about the chakra system into diagnosing and treating patients, I had better results. This is because psycho-spiritual understanding helps to illuminate the true cause of health and illness as much as a strictly medical and musculoskeletal assessment. Energy medicine has a real place in health and healing because long before problems show up in the physical body, they have been percolating in the mental/emotional/spiritual body. Energy creates physicality just as thoughts create reality. Buddha says, "Every human being is the author of his own health or disease." I believe this to be true.

Energetically, I was suffering in the second chakra. Since adolescence I had terrible menstrual problems, severe endometriosis, fibroids and ultimately, metastatic breast cancer in both ovaries. My history and psychology affected my biology.

The chakras continue up the body to the top of the head. The third chakra is located at the solar plexus and relates to self-esteem. The expression, "I feel it in my gut" or "I have a gut feeling about this," is connected to third chakra wisdom and is usually accurate if we listen. The third chakra relates to the organs of upper digestion like stomach, gallbladder, liver, pancreas and small intestines. It also relates to part of the kidneys and the adrenal glands that cap the kidneys and help us deal with stress. The adrenals are our "fight or flight" organs; they are also responsible for the production of endorphins, the neurotransmitters responsible for what is commonly referred to as "runners high." This is also the area from which anger can arise. In Chinese medicine, liver is related to anger. It is also tied in with feeling unfulfilled or that life isn't what we had hoped. These feelings can cause liver qi (energy) rising or excess liver qi and anger will arise. Of course, anger turned inward is depression and we call this liver qi "misting the heart" in Chinese medicine.

The fourth chakra, the heart chakra, is located at the breasts in the center of the body. The heart represents love that is the center of our lives. This chakra relates to the heart and lungs and is important because so much emotion is felt and held here. The heart energy houses the capacity for love and forgiveness as well as hate and blame. In the course of an hour or a day, we experience many emotions of the heart. Over years, these feelings can get stuck and accumulate in our bodies and we don't know how to release or express them. Women have a particularly difficult time asking for their heart's desire, especially self-sufficient women. We are capable of nurturing and giving love to others but less proficient at receiving love. Resentment builds up because of this inability to receive love and then heart problems begin to develop. It is no surprise then, that heart disease is the leading cause of death in women over forty. This statistic intrigues me. By our forties, most women have been tending to husbands, children, and careers for many years; we have a tendency to put ourselves on the back burner in order to take care of other demanding issues at hand. I think women get so entrenched in our instinctual maternal and nurturing role that we don't notice that we have lost our ability to receive love. In fact, many of us feel undeserving about taking what we need. Often we have, unknowingly, trained our children and our husbands to accept our love without feeling any need to reciprocate. I don't think it ever occurs to my children that I need love and nurturing as much as they do or that I sometimes feel sad and lonely. I don't think they imagine me completely depleted. They think of me as larger than life, the one who gives and needs nothing in return. Like women everywhere, I gave them the message that I am a self-sufficient woman. But that simply isn't true; we are social animals and we need each other. We need to receive love and acknowledgement or we will suffer physically; we may even die of a broken heart.

One of the more interesting phenomenon that I noticed in my practice involved women in their late 40's whose children had recently left home. Practically overnight, women who were suffering from empty nest syndrome began drinking. Within a year, they became serious drinkers who were unable to control their drinking. I found this fascinating because I had assumed that alcoholism would have appeared earlier in life and if it hadn't manifested until mid-life, it couldn't be a serious problem. But I was wrong. Nearly half of these women joined AA and became active in reaching out to help other women. Many women don't know what to do with themselves when they haven't found other outlets for what comes naturally, for what they have been doing for the first half of their lives - nurturing others.

I wondered: what do we do with all this heart energy? Nobody seems to want the best that we have to offer – our love. Our children are gone and our partners are busy at work. I learned a lot from these women and prepared myself well in anticipation of my own empty nest. I began new projects prior to each one of my children's leaving for college. But, after they left, I still felt lost and empty from around five o'clock in the evening until I went to bed. I felt a deep ache for my children that lasted for about two years. I never dreamed I would feel such pain. I thought my life was full, that I would hardly miss my children and if I did, I would simply go visit them. My natural tendency toward introversion was more obvious when I didn't have children to pull me out of myself and falling back into that behavior felt uncomfortable and lonely. Oh, the heart, with all its emotions, is such a marvelous teacher.

The fourth chakra also relates to the lung and, when imbalanced, can indicate sadness - a deep weeping inside the soul. Lung disease is rampant in our society among people of all ages: asthma, emphysema and COPD, and lung cancer. I often encounter sadness in children with asthma, and I see it in the faces of my older patients – especially those whose lungs are so diseased they require oxygen tanks. It's heartbreaking.

Learning how to manage our feelings more effectively would be a formidable step toward becoming healthier, happier people. I am convinced that my failure to manage my own emotions in a healthy way led to my heart attack, which occurred exactly one year before I was diagnosed with left breast cancer. My heart was broken - literally and figuratively. I believe I contributed to my own heartbreak by habitually expressing to myself and others: I am self-sufficient; I don't need anything, including love. I have misrepresented myself to avoid intimacy; I have been an imposter in my own life. Identifying this behavior was a beginning, as was the willingness to change. But knowing that I could not be completely healthy until I moved through this fear and embraced intimacy was the real driving force. Ultimately, though, the comfort and joy of being close and connected in my relationships, being intimate, was its own reward. I simply felt better, more whole.

Health and being healthy is multi-faceted and I initially thought that living a healthy lifestyle – diet, exercise, meditation, fresh air and a wonderful career – would be enough to keep me healthy. But it wasn't. It is the emotions and the energy underlying these emotions that have a huge influence on our health.

The fifth chakra - the throat chakra - has to do with our will, our voice and speaking our truth. It is located just above the manubrium which is the little bone above the sternum. People with chronic throat problems can have problems finding their voice and speaking out. Often, our will gets stuck between the heart and the head and we end up speechless. In other words, we may know what we desire deep in our hearts and we may know intellectually what we "should" do, but we may not have the will to make a choice - follow our heart or follow our head. When I see chronic sore throats, recurring strep infections, mononucleosis, temporal mandibular joint pain, neck and thyroid problems in my office, I tend to see a person who struggles with asserting his or her will. I find that for me, and perhaps for many of us, the heart is more attuned to who we are and what we need. I imagine how our lives would change if we found the courage to regularly listen and speak from the heart.

In the Catholic faith tradition, February third is the feast day of St. Blaise when the congregation receives the blessing of the throat. St. Blaise lived in the 4th century and was revered as a gifted physician who later became a Roman Catholic bishop. Because of religious persecution, he fled and lived in prayer in a cave. He was captured and on his way to prison, he cured a young boy who was choking on a fish bone stuck in his throat. While in prison, a woman expressed her gratitude to him for having helped her by bringing him white candles every day so that he could read in the darkness of his cell; thus, the priest performs the blessing of the throat with white candles. Placing the crossed candles at the throat, he says, "Through the intercession of St. Blaise, bishop and martyr, may God deliver you from every disease of the throat and from every other illness, in the name of the Father, and of the Son, and of the Holy

Spirit." I always evoke this blessing when I work with the second chakra because I loved it when I was growing up. It always came just in the nick of time – winter had been going on too long, kids were stuck inside with the heat on and colds and flu abounded. Our physical bodies needed help. Now I imagine that this blessing also applies to our spiritual tongue, throat, and voice that are crying out for the grace to speak our truth and assert our will. I also believe this blessing gives us the grace to avoid profanity, gossip, and unkind remarks. Saint James said, "If a man who does not control his tongue imagines that he is devout, he is self-deceived; his worship is pointless" (1:26). I strive to remember that speaking ill of others is as harmful to my health as swallowing nails.

The sixth chakra is located at the brow line and is often referred to as the third eye. It is the seat of wisdom and intuition. This energy center relates to the brain, eyes, ears, nose and the pituitary and pineal glands. We often doubt our intuition even when it is guiding us in the direction we are meant to go. When we ignore this guidance, sinus infections, vision problems and tingling in the ears can result. In many Eastern philosophies, the third eye is a sacred passageway through which grace and God enter our lives.

The seventh chakra is located at the top of the head and is referred to as the crown chakra. Energetically, it involves our relationship with the Divine. Physically, it relates to the neuromusculoskeletal system. Mystics, saints, and enlightened beings live largely from this energy center, but most of us just pass through it from time to time. For much of my life, I have longed to fully open to this holy light.

The energy of each chakra corresponds to a color. The base chakra, or first chakra, is the color red. The colors associated with the second through seventh chakra are gradations of orange, yellow, green, blue, purple and lavender. Some people are able to see these colors.

The chakra system is a brilliant way to identify problems areas in the body and to then look at the psycho-spiritual energy associated with these areas. As an acupuncturist, I could easily affect these areas by either increasing or dispersing energy flow using needles and moxa. Understanding the chakras brought another dimension to my practice and made it more interesting for me as a practitioner and for my patients who could participate more fully in their healing.

My practice was moving along effortlessly. However, my teenage children were moving along far too quickly and not at all effortlessly for me. When they began pulling away, as teenagers do, I began doing the same. I didn't feel wanted or needed. If we are doing our job as a parent effectively then we must allow our children to individuate. This is critical to their ultimate health and happiness as fully functioning adults in society. I knew this intellectually but it was a challenge for me to loosen my grip and allow them to fly. It also seems that if we, as parents, aren't willing to loosen the grip when the child is ready to move on, we run the risk of obstructing their exquisite and timely flight. I have seen this with overprotective parents who disallow their children to explore life independently and the teen becomes fearful. Then the opportunity to test the waters with their peers is lost and they withdraw. I have also seen the opposite: no boundaries or discipline with subsequent chaos in the life of the young one.

Every spring the song swallows come to nest just outside our sunroom sliding doors. She and her mate spend a few days busily collecting branches, dog and cat hair and cotton from the cottontails to make their nest. Before long, she has laid her eggs and begins her long wait for her chicks to arrive. Finally, the little baby chicks begin to peck through those mottled eggs until they break out and begin their journey outside the protective shell. Then, it is the feeding and waiting game: all day long those little guys squeak and squeal for food. It appears as though mom and dad take turns with this chore. After a few weeks, the parents await their chicks' first flight. I have watched as mama sparrow encourages her little ones to take their first steps and then fly. It seems that every year there is one chick that is reluctant to leave the nest and hangs back. My husband and I begin to quietly encourage the ill-prepared chick to muster the courage and take the leap. The parents won't leave until the last chick has left the nest so they keep coming back to check on him and encourage him to fly. They flutter about, reprimanding the baby swallow for not facing his destiny. It usually only takes a day or two after his siblings have left for the final chick to leave the nest. John and I are full of angst that he won't find the courage to leave. So we wait with bated breath until he happily flies off.

It is the same with our children. They must leave the nest and become their own individual beings. They can always return to the human nest as an independent part of the whole. That way, they can walk through life confident and capable with the knowledge of who they are apart from their family as well as a part of their family. We have all had to do this; with varying degrees of difficulty and/or ease. Yet, as the mother hen to my precious chicks, I found their flight particularly difficult and lonely.

It was an interesting phenomenon in our home when I was in my mid to late forties and my children became teenagers . My hormones were waning and my children's were cranked up and we weren't exactly communicating. I wanted them to toe the line and they wanted to have fun. While my tolerance for nonsense was low, their tolerance for a meddling mom was even lower. They used to ask, regularly, "How do you always know what we are up to, even before we actually are? None of the other moms has a clue." My pet answer was, "Your guardian angel tells my guardian angel, who then tells me, and I am now telling you, you can't do this." I was referring to alcohol and pot. And it is true; many of the other moms didn't have a clue. But, being who I am, I had to know what was going on with my children at all times. Plus, I had made that pact with God that I would be the best Mom I could, if He/She would let us live through that hurricane. My husband is not a disciplinarian and he can be unbelievably naive. It was inconceivable to me that a grown man could be that naïve. But, in fairness, he was never exposed to life the way I was and the way my kids were. I also think it was important to him that the children like and respect him. That no longer was as important to me as having children behave in a way that I felt was healthy, safe and honorable. So, we played good cop, bad cop and I was always the bad cop; albeit one with heart.

These were hard times because I wouldn't, I couldn't, back down and I was driving my children crazy, particularly my son. He felt that a little alcohol and pot on the weekends was fine. Fear had me in knots: I was afraid that marijuana would cause amotivational syndrome and my children would become like people I knew in the 60's who have still not found their way. And, statistics point to marijuana use leading to more serious, devastating drug use. Never before in my life had I had so little control over what was happening around me and it was breaking my heart. Kieran was diagnosed with ADD in his junior year in high school (like so many in our county) and it was suggested that he take adderall. This would not have been my choice, but I left it up to him. He very sadly said, "Mom, I don't really have a choice; without it I can't focus." So, on this drug, my tall, very thin son lost twenty-five pounds, which he could ill afford, and he was unable to sleep at night. He hated the side effects of taking adderal; weed was his solution to this dilemma – it helped by increasing his appetite and it eased his sleeplessness. Yet, I continued my quest to rid him of this behavior. I tried everything: therapists, four-week Outward Bound programs, bribery, everything - until I gave up.

My daughter was much easier with regard to substance abuse. Like her mother, she enjoys being in complete control so anything that dampened that control, was short lived. She was not an angel but she was responsible.

We were being pulled in different directions, my children and I. I resorted to my old behavior of running away because I was frustrated and sad and I felt like I had no control over what was happening in my life. I had been put out to pasture, not just by my children but by my husband who felt I was overreacting.

Between my career, my household, and chauffeuring kids who didn't really want me involved in their lives, I was exhausted. Which is why, at age forty-five, I was bone tired - completely spent, both emotionally and physically. I was hoping to find something that would lift me up, bring passion back into my soul and I figured the most acceptable outlet for a professional, married woman with children was more education. I convinced myself and my family that in order to be a better, more cutting edge doctor, I needed to take more courses, both in my field and in the realm of spirituality. Many of these classes were not offered anywhere close by, so I began traveling all over the world.

When I boarded that plane to wherever I was heading, leaving my life as I knew it behind, I took a deep breath, relaxed into myself, and felt immediate rejuvenation. I was free and for the next few days it was all about me: my own bed, my own room; I could order whatever I wanted for breakfast and dinner, or I could skip dinner and have popcorn and watch a movie, I could stay up reading with the light on, until 2 or 3 a.m. if I wanted to, or I could go to bed at 8:00; it was totally up to me. And it was pure bliss. I took every course imaginable during this time of my life which lasted about five years and I learned a lot. I think I became a better doctor. I completed my acupuncture curriculum and licensure and I staved off depression and hopelessness. I missed my family when I was separated from them but when I was home, I felt my job was to make sure everyone was happy, everything was taken care of, and that life was chugging along smoothly. I was unable to claim what I needed to keep me running on full instead of empty. This was new territory for me because my life appeared to be incredibly abundant; I had more than I ever wanted, yet I felt empty inside.

Now, when I talk about this with friends and I observe other women and men, I realize it is fairly universal; we approach our mid-forties on a path we began in our mid- twenties, but many of us never stopped long enough to make a soul correction. It stands to reason that our deepest longings and desires in our twenties will look very different in our forties and fifties. It's like trying on our old favorite jeans from college that used to fit us perfectly - every thing about them was exactly right. But now, twenty years and twenty pounds later, we can hardly breathe in them. We are bursting at the seams and all we want is to get out of them.

It has been called a crisis; this soul longing that wanders into our lives at its midpoint. We have seen it manifested in many ways, slightly different between the sexes, but not always. Women gravitate towards self-help books, workshops, spas, cosmetic surgery, horses, gurus, redecorating homes, excess exercising and anything and everything that will bring us back to ourselves. Men seem to find newer, slicker and more exciting models of cars and women; new big toys like boats and tractors, extreme sports, and time in the wild. Sometimes this crisis involves new careers, excessive volunteerism, withdrawal and/or drinking too much. And, of course, none of it keeps the emptiness at bay. In America, we don't talk much about this transformative time or how to navigate these choppy waters. We simply say, as we roll our eyes and grimace, "Wow! He must be in a major mid-life crisis. Look at that car and my God, his arm candy looks young enough to be his granddaughter!" And this may be true but not helpful. What would be helpful is if we had elders who could guide us through these transitional times; who encouraged us to give ourselves space for emerging thoughts and feelings that are both unfamiliar and uncomfortable, but ultimately exhilarating. Then, perhaps we could go to the edge without fear, knowing that this is another opportunity in our life that is replete with possibilities and gifts.

I could have used guidance then. Perhaps I would not have felt like a selfish, ungrateful malcontent; I would have been gentler with myself if I had known I was birthing a new and enlarged vision of myself and my life. Now, I know better and I hope when the time comes, I can help my children approach mid-life with grace and gratitude. But, I didn't know that at the time, so I began running for my life.

Running away was my modus operandi: I ran to boarding school to get away from feeling disconnected from my peers at Taipei American school, I ran to Europe to get away from my family of origin and claim my own life, I ran and ran until I was diagnosed with cancer; then, there was no place to hide. When I look back on my life I realize I could have saved myself a lot of expense and traveling time if I had realized that you cannot run away from yourself. We can, however, run towards ourselves with arms and heart wide open. This is what I have been trying to do since my cancer diagnosis. I do still travel, but not nearly as frequently, or as far, or for as long a time. I am healing from this need to be apart or away to feel complete. I am learning to say "no" even when the person to whom I am saying "no" looks at me as though I am a heartless, three headed monster. My self-concept is not nearly as entangled with those whom I love. I am resting a lot even when those around me are all a-flutter with activity and productivity; I no longer feel the need to be productive to not look like a slacker. I am touching in with my heart and my soul to make sure I am being true and authentic. That is how I am now able to love more deeply and completely with no resentment.

I also know that no one can add to or subtract from who I am unless I give them that power and, contrary to what I used to think, most people have a full plate with their own lives and they don't really want to run my life, too. I think when we feel "less than," as I did and do still sometimes, we make the people we love the most, our spouses in particular, wrong for wanting too much from us. This usually is about us wanting more from ourselves because we are still trying to be good enough. It is this mirroring onto my spouse that kept me running while all the while he only wanted my happiness.

I am learning to come home to my heart and allow it to be big enough to encompass me. This life we live is our story in the making and if we honor our heart and our soul, and relax into our lives, we will live our lives with integrity, authenticity and joy. That is what I have been learning these past few years. Perhaps it was this turn – the turn towards self-love – that I thought I had missed and was now looking for so diligently.

In this speech, Oriah Mountain Dreamer speaks eloquently about being true to ourselves and to those we love:

> It doesn't interest me what you do for a living. I want to know what you ache for, and if you dare to dream of meeting your heart's longing
>
> It doesn't interest me what planets are squaring your moon. I want to know if you have touched the center of your own sorrow, if you have been opened by life's betrayals or have become shriveled and closed from fear of further pain.
>
> I want to know if you can sit with pain, mine or your own, without moving to hide it or fade it or fix it.

I want to know if you can be with joy, mine or your own; if you can dance with wildness and let the ecstasy fill you to the tips of your fingers and toes without cautioning us to be careful, be realistic, or to remember the limitations of being human

It doesn't interest me if the story you're telling me is true. I want to know if you can disappoint another to be true to yourself; if you can bear the accusation of betrayal and not betray your own soul.

I want to know if you can be faithful and therefore be trustworthy.

I want to know if you can see beauty even when it is not pretty everyday, and if you can source your life from God's presence.

I want to know if you can live with failure, yours and mine, and still stand on the edge of a lake and shout to the silver of the full moon, "yes!"

It doesn't interest me to know where you live or how much money you have. I want to know if you can get up after the night of grief and despair, weary and bruised to the bone, and do what needs to be done for the children.

It doesn't interest me who you are, how you came to be here. I want to know if you will stand in the center of the fire with me and not shrink back.

It doesn't interest me where or what or with whom you have studied. I want to know what sustains you from the inside when all else fails.

I want to know if you can be alone with yourself, and if you truly like the company you keep in the empty moments.

Oriah Mountain Dreamer, Native American Elder

PART TWO

"Looking Forward"

CHAPTER TEN

Moving On

You walking, your footprints are
the road, and nothing else;
there is no road, walker,
you make the road by walking.
By walking you make the road,
And when you look backward,
You see the path you
Never will step on again.
Walker, there is no road,
Only wind trails in the sea.

Antonio Machado

While my reflections on early childhood, adolescence, young adulthood, motherhood and mid-life have been curative and cathartic, it has also been a detour from determining a treatment path. My initial hypothesis that I must have taken a wrong turn on my life path now seems terribly naïve. The intricate latticework of paths that I have walked throughout my lifetime is gently converging into one little path leading to my life at this moment. I don't think all these roads go anywhere, they just bring you home. My life experiences, while not all pretty, have been rich and profoundly helpful in shaping who I have become. It had been my innocent hope, or perhaps a fantasy, that this process would be a simple exercise in identification – that I would have an "aha" moment when I saw the life experience labeled "wrong turn" or "cancer causing agent," (like saccharin) and I could simply correct it and the cancer would disappear forever. I assumed it would be straightforward like identifying the gene on a chromosome that determines if a child will have blue eyes. I had been willing to open the Pandora's Box of my life to identify and examine all possibilities - some fun, some silly and some more serious: perhaps Catholic School had ruined me; perhaps I should have been more wild and cavalier. Maybe instead of walking down the aisle to say "I do," I should have said, "I can't, I don't know how to do marriage, it is just too much." Perhaps instead of being a practicing physician, I should have owned a horse farm in Vermont. Or maybe it was that watershed moment when my son announced, in sixth grade, that he didn't want to be like his mom and dad because we didn't look like we were having any fun, and all we did was work, and he was just giving us a heads up that he had decided that fun was important. So he would no longer be the top of his class, or the best athlete on the soccer field or on the basketball court because that wasn't who he wanted to be. My

God, his voice hadn't even changed yet. But what did change, after that very telling moment, was his school attendance. He went from being sick eighteen to twenty days a year to not missing a single day of school for the next six years. The stress was gone and his immune system was much happier, as was he.

This was a pivotal moment for our family and I was deeply grateful that my son had found his voice. I was shocked at the unconscious message we had been sending our children: fun wasn't nearly as important as performance, either in work or in play. In truth, I really didn't believe that, but that was clearly the message I was sending. My son saw two lives void of passion and sadly, he was right. Equally sad is the fact that, had I chosen to look at that back then, I wouldn't be staring it in the face ten years later.

It isn't one or two or even ten separate incidents, it is how we hold our lives; how we walk through them and the energy and attitudes we bring to them. It is the heart or its lack that infuses our lives. Happiness truly is an inside job. It is not what is out there but what is in here, inside our heart, soul and spirit. It is very, very close; no need to travel the world over to find answers; just take that very long, arduous journey eighteen inches down from your head to your heart. There you will find your answers. It is not nearly as glamorous as going on a vision quest or spending five weeks in Tibet to circle the Sacred Mountain, but it is as wonderful and challenging a journey as you will ever make. When most of our decisions are made from our head, without inviting the heart in, we are simply out of balance. Our head encourages us to set goals that we believe will ultimately make us happy and successful. If, however, our heart is not in it, like mine wasn't, we become lost, disconnected, and soul-less. Reaching our goals is no longer meaningful but we are still reaching, largely out of habit. That is what causes illness. I know that and it is interesting how I can see this in others' lives more clearly than in my own.

My life had become heart-less, empty and devoid of passion. I didn't know why or when, I just knew that deep inside of me, I had changed and my life hadn't. I was a square peg in a round hole. But the thought of changing the way I walked through life was too disruptive, too overwhelming and too exhausting to think about. However, as we all know, once we plant the seed of change, it begins to grow and there is no stopping it. For the last few years, I had been feeling a slow, yet increasingly urgent wave of change washing over me. I knew it was time and the cancer gave me the impetus. Searching through my past was simply a lovely diversion from my illness and what I must do to reclaim my health, passion and joy.

There is deep, steadfast denial in the process leading up to acknowledging that your doctor has given you an accurate diagnosis. There are visits to other doctors at other facilities for second and third opinions. I had thought that I might return to Houston for my treatment because M.D. Anderson is considered one of the best oncology hospitals in the world. My oncologist said, "Jacqui, cancer research is not a secret. Research is available to anyone as soon as it has been published.

So, if you decide to go to M.D. Anderson, know that they don't have any secrets that we are not privy to here in Connecticut." To a large extent, that is true, but a friend of mine at M.D. Anderson said that every 90 seconds, new information replaces the old information. Research is changing that fast. I wasn't convinced that this cutting edge research was being done here in Connecticut nor was I sure that it was being implemented. However, the treatments were still current and there is a lot to be said for being treated in your own backyard by dear friends. So, I stayed.

On the way home from visiting the breast surgeon I had chosen from among several, I was overwhelmed by my new reality. Pollyanna had to be put aside; it was time to realize the gravity of the situation. I had to take a leap of faith from information gathering to beginning treatment. As a doctor, I was very objective about the research and collection of treatment options: I took copious notes, asked numerous questions, verified everything I was told on the Internet and called friends who had been through it. I was every physician's nightmare. However, it kept me removed from the reality of the situation until I could deal with it. The problem was, I did not want to end this process. I was comfortable and in my element. Once the talking was over and the action had to begin, I was devastated, truly pathetic and broken to the very core of my being. That happened the day we left the breast surgeon's office in Hartford after receiving all the information concerning the gravity of the cancer, size of the tumor and necessity of major surgery.

Driving home, I couldn't talk, I couldn't cry or get angry, and for the second time in my life, I couldn't find the silver lining. I wanted the world to go away and I wanted my husband to go away. I tried to become very small and invisible. I reclined the passenger seat as far as it would go, I rolled toward the passenger door and turned my back completely towards my husband. Then I pulled my knees up to my chest, and laid with my head digging into the shoulder strap of the seat belt so that I could feel something, anything, and I begged God to take away the previous hour of my life, to please make it not be so. And, I blamed my husband for not loving me well enough.

Many of us in complementary medicine believe that left breast cancer in women, and men alike, relates to issues of the heart. And because we tend to project onto the people we love the most our hurt feelings and make them wrong, I was blaming my suffering on my husband, building a case that he was unable to love me the way that I needed to be loved, that if he had I wouldn't have cancer. It couldn't possibly have been my fault, I reasoned, because I had done everything right. Hadn't I been in therapy for most of my life, shouldn't I have handled my "heart issues" long ago? I caught myself in a trap of my own making, so I lay there like an animal in the wild that is being stalked and doesn't move a muscle for fear that she will be found and subsequently, devoured. I was trying desperately to disappear.

Later, I thought again about this heart energy. My husband was born and raised in New England, second generation Irish. New England and the Irish – the combination doesn't leave much hope for warm and fuzzy. John personifies New England reserve: he is a man of few words, he is not a hugger or touchy feely, he rarely raises his voice and he is always in control. Growing up in eastern Connecticut, the Martins were one of the few Catholic families in the small town of Scotland. I have often heard the story of his grandfather's family driving a horse and buggy to a neighboring town to attend Sunday Mass. Nothing could deter these old Irish Catholics from attending Sunday Mass, no matter the distance or inconvenience. It was their duty and responsibility; hard work was the gauge of a man. When John was young, his mother was ill for many years and died when he was fifteen. I am told that his mother was stern, no-nonsense, and brilliantly frugal. She was a published writer and heavily involved with politics. The family was particularly proud of the fact that she was invited to President Kennedy's inaugural ball. The fourth of six children, John probably got lost in the shuffle during his mother's illness and death. I imagine there wasn't much coddling and stroking going on during that very difficult time for his family.

My mother, on the other hand, ruled from her heart. It is a testament to her wisdom that my father, with an MBA from Wharton School of Business, deferred to her in decisions about finance, schooling and real estate. Rumi, a fourteenth century Persian poet, says that true intelligence comes from the heart not the mind. I am infinitely grateful to my mother for her wholeheartedness and for passing it on to me.

While I received my mother's heart, it was defended. So, my beloved and I met on common ground with hearts not so willing to be opened and poured out freely. As I lay there in a fetal position, I realized that I had wanted to change the marriage rules. I was ready to give and receive love more fully and openly, however, I forgot to tell my husband which is why I was blaming him now for not loving me properly. And it is unfair to change the foundation of an institution without consulting other members. This was one of the many blessings that came with breast cancer; I was now eager to change. Time softens, trust builds, needs change, and love opens the heart. Children come into our lives, break open our hearts and we can walk proudly and blissfully through the bars and chains that have imprisoned us. Ironically, we never see it coming. So, I felt that to get well and stay well, John and I would have to face ourselves and our habitual way of being. Withholding love - consciously or unconsciously - never works in a committed relationship.

I have learned a lot from my dog Dudley about love. Every time he sees me, it's as if it's for the first time and he has been waiting for me for his entire life. This is especially true of the mornings. Dudley sleeps just outside our bedroom door and when I open the door in the morning to greet him, his entire body is wagging and his eyes look moony, like a teenager hopelessly in love. He can't contain himself. He runs back to his basket of toys to get something to chew on, like a pacifier, because the moment is too intense. He knows he can't jump, but his paws are dancing in very high step, almost coming off the floor as he wraps his 116-pound body around me in a big hug. He is giddy with love and a very contented sound escapes him which sounds like a combination of relief and comfort: she is here, once again, to start the day, it's a miracle! That's true love. I decided that I wanted to be like that and I decided it was time to choose a cancer treatment.

Allopathic treatment for cancer is one of the most brutal treatments and, the worse the cancer, the more brutal the treatment. Nonetheless, it also seems to be the most successful. There are no conclusive studies that confirm the effectiveness of alternative treatments for cancer, such as diet, mind over matter, spiritual healing, supplement regiments, gurus, meditation, homeopathy, and so on. However, a pilot study out of Duke University Medical Center took a random sample of three groups of patients to measure the efficacy of prayer. They concluded that those patients assigned to receive prayer and did in fact receive it, appeared to fare far better than those told they wouldn't receive prayers, and those told they would receive prayers, but did not. This significant study caught the attention of the scientific community. In general, however, alternative approaches to cancer treatment require a huge commitment to the unknown and a giant leap of faith because you take sole responsibility for your own healing. There is no day-to-day gauge of how you are doing. I weighed the research, looked at the side effects and long-term ramifications of each treatment and then I prayed for guidance and clarity in making my decision. I also honored my gut, which is the squeaky wheel in my life. For the first time, I relinquished responsibility and deferred, with some negotiations, to my oncologist, who became a great source of comfort. I have known Jedd for many years but had never seen the "caretaker" side of him. My respect and love for him grew exponentially as he encouraged, explained, and honored my questioning and decision-making.

Invasive lobular carcinoma accounts for about 5-10% of all breast cancer and it likes to metastasize to the meninges, serosal surfaces, ovaries and retroperitoneam. The meninges are the three membranes or linings that surround the brain and spinal cord; serosal surfaces are the areas where there is a lining of a body part, for example the lining of the small and large intestines; ovaries are the female sexual glands that lie on either side of the pelvis; and the retroperitoneum is the area that sits behind the clear lining or sac that holds the organs of the abdominal-pelvic area.

The severity of a cancer is determined by factors such as margins, estrogen and progesterone receptors, proliferation index, HER2Neu (sounds like a star wars character), size, lymphovascular invasion and grade. Ideally, you want a clear margin. If a tumor is responsive to estrogen and progesterone, the oncologist will want to shut down any hormonal activity. The proliferation index relates to the percentage of cells that are actively growing. Size is simply the size of the tumor in centimeters. Grade is determined under a microscope and has to do with cellular differentiation. And, lymphovascular invasion refers to whether or not the cancer has spread to regional lymph nodes. All of these factors determine the stage of your cancer and thus your treatment options. My cancer was Stage IIB.

In my twenty-five years of practicing, many patients had told me about these indicators in great detail, with regard to their cancer, and I had always listened intently. But when it came to my own diagnosis, I didn't want to become too intimate with these details because they frightened me. Being the patient instead of the doctor was a new and painful experience. My empathy for illness grew geometrically after that.

I chose to start with chemotherapy to shrink the tumor, hoping I would be a candidate for a lumpectomy instead of a mastectomy. After three months, it was clear that I would need a mastectomy; a surgeon was chosen and a November date was scheduled. I didn't want to wake up following surgery sans breast and I didn't want anything artificial put into my body, like saline or silicon, so I currently had one choice: a tram flap surgery. In 2002, this surgery was considered state of the arts but it is barbaric. The surgeon makes an incision from one hip to the other and he removes the rectus abdominus muscle from its insertion and brings it across and up to my new breast for circulation. My new breast is formed from the abdominal tissue that is pushed up beneath my skin to my chest wall to form my breast. While it was a difficult recovery, the advantage is that, when I awoke, I had a flat belly and a smooth scoop of vanilla ice cream for a breast. This is good for morale, which is good for healing.

My husband and daughter were waiting for me to return to the hospital room following my surgery. They waited and waited and I was finally wheeled into the room four hours later than when they were told to expect me. My husband is still convinced that something went terribly wrong, though when he asked, he was told that my surgery took longer than expected. John is intuitive and I suspect something did go wrong but we will never know for sure. The look on my husband and daughter's faces when I was wheeled into that room was unbearable: they were drained of all color, their eyes were soft and moist and sad. They were both frightened and relieved, and deeply concerned for me. I felt sad and guilty that I had put them through this torment. And, because of her fear and concern for me, my seventeen-year- old daughter would not leave my bedside. Seeing me in a hospital bed hooked up to a multitude of tubes, was too much for her to bear. She wanted to come close and she wanted to hang back, but mostly she wanted to assure me that I was okay. So, she asked the nurse for a cot and set herself up in my room. Throughout the night, whenever the medical equipment beeped, she got out of bed, went to the nurses' station and dragged someone back to take care of the situation. I didn't sleep at all because I was worried about her and she didn't sleep out of fear that each time the machines started beeping it meant I was dying. I can't express how grateful I was to Meghan for being with me that night. I weep every time I think of how difficult that must have been for her and how much I needed her. I abhor being medicated because of my need to be in control. I would never have asked my daughter to stay with me; that she chose to on her own was a beautiful gift.

I arranged to be released from the hospital four days ahead of schedule. I was told I could go home as soon as I passed gas, walked the length of the floor, and had someone at home to look after me. I had a mission and I worked hard to accomplish it by the third day. We rented a hospital bed and put it in the library of our home and John and Meghan split nursing duty: John stayed home until eleven a.m. and Meghan switched her high school schedule so she could be home by eleven.

My daughter is not a touchy-feely child, she is excruciatingly clear about her personal space and she will never be a nurse. But she did an amazing job of taking care of me during my recovery: she checked my vitals, brought me meals and medication, kept me company and emptied my drainage tubes. We still laugh about her approach to performing the dirty deed of emptying the blood from the drains and measuring it. She would announce, from an adjoining room, that it was time to empty the drains and I could hear in her voice that she was already holding her nose! This was her precious way of bracing against too much closeness.

It is amazing what we teach our children simply through example, no discussion. I suspect this is particularly true of mothers and daughters with respect to care giving because every morning during the first six weeks of my recovery, Meghan got up early and basically assumed my role: she got up, showered, came downstairs and fed the animals, emptied the dishwasher, filled it back up, made me breakfast and brought it to me and only then did she stop long enough to say good-morning and sit for a visit. Then she went to school. I was astounded and amused that she had internalized my morning routine because, as she was growing up, I had finished this part of my morning ritual before she had come down for breakfast. I was so proud of her I felt I might burst.

Following eight weeks of recovery, I resumed chemotherapy. I negotiated the number of treatments down to about seventy percent of what my oncologist recommended because I knew my body couldn't take any more than that.

After many months of research and speaking to three different radiologists, I made an educated and intuitive decision to refuse radiation. The reason was simple: radiation is permanent, as is the damage it incurs; one can only receive radiation once in the same area so if cancer returns in that area, it would not be an option. I chose to save it for a later time, should it be necessary. I simply didn't want to be radiated.

Chemotherapy brought me to my knees; I had never been so sick. Sometimes we have to be down on our knees to stop, listen, and feel our feelings. Every morning, I sat with God and asked for strength to get through the day. And every day I received more than I needed. Walking through life with cancer delivered me to the best part of myself. I became softer, more humble, more inward, and more allowing of help. In fact, learning to receive has helped me to correct a life-long imbalance.

Two years prior to my diagnosis, a dear and wise friend suggested I pay attention to my tendency to put out and not take in. Sensing the truth of her insight, I began a meditative practice. First thing in the morning and last thing at night, I said aloud, "I am receiving," with a heart-felt smile on my face and hands opened and lifted up in a gesture of receiving. While I couldn't see any evidence of this practice actually "working," the real proof came shortly after my surgery and chemotherapy. News travels fast in a small town, especially if you are a female doctor sporting a shiny, perfectly bald head. Gifts started pouring in: cards, flowers, hats, scarves, jewelry, false eye-lashes, baseball caps, prayer cards, phone calls and delicious, well balanced, vegetarian dinners. Every night for six weeks, one, two, sometimes three dinners would show up. I would have been horrified by all this generosity and attention if I hadn't been practicing receiving. I was thrilled and I loved this receiving business: Every day was like my birthday. It is never too late to learn this beautiful lesson.

Paradoxically, while my body was suffering, my spirit was dwelling in a deep and rich experience of the sacred - the soft, sweet, supportive place where I could simply be. I recognized this place because I had longed for it for so long. Just being: it happened effortlessly when I gave up trying.

It is said that children live in the spirit realm more than on the earth plane for their first seven years of life. After that, they become more earthbound, more grounded. During that time, they may have magical friends and magical conversations. I was always delighted to see that shimmering light in my children's eyes as they seemed to shift back and forth from one realm to another. That is how I understood what was happening to me: I was shifting my attention from the pain and suffering in my body to the spiritual realm where I found comfort and strength. I spent many hours a day in meditation and sacred conversation and knew that I was changed. I experienced an increased capacity to appreciate both the human and non-human world.

I wondered about illness and death in the animal world; whether they felt emotions as pain increased. It seemed to me that suffering has to do with the human condition. One end of the pain continuum is well defined like a broken toe. Historically, there is a short healing period, no serious pain, not a lot of investment in the diagnosis but some aggravation. At the other end of the continuum, like with cancer, the psychology of pain enters the equation and we add emotions like fear, anxiety, hopelessness and sympathy. Our resolve that we will heal quickly and effortlessly breaks down and fear climbs in and it seems to me that is when suffering comes in. The individual suffers and we suffer collectively for anyone diagnosed with cancer. I felt empathy for others and I felt their empathy for me but I didn't want to linger too long here. I felt it would be better for me to move down the continuum away from "cancer" and any labeled illnesses and concentrate not on the illness but on healing; to give less energy to the diagnosis. That was helpful.

My family became very protective and solicitous of me and in many ways I had never felt happier. During that year of intense treatment, my relationship with family and friends grew deeper; mysteriously, the walls between us came down, defenses melted away and I experienced being deliciously alive and fully in the present moment. That was the agony and ecstasy of my life at that time. I had been other-directed but with cancer everything changed. Then every day was simply about getting through the day; I had no excess energy for anything else. So, I became a witness, an appreciator of what was going on around me. I became quieter inside by necessity and it felt lovely. Many subtle changes were happening without my even realizing it. Some days, I needed to do acupuncture on myself in between patients in order to dispel nausea or to increase energy. This made it possible for me to keep working, which made me happy.

It was lovely receiving so much love and attention and it was healing, but I couldn't help wondering if all the incoming love and concern would soon wane and I would revert back to my familiar caretaking mode and this mysterious and transformational interval would just fade away. I vowed to stay awake to what having cancer forced me to face.

It is simply impossible to be everything to everybody – I knew that intellectually. Yet, I became aware of being constantly tyrannized by mental pictures of how I wanted things to be; like how to gently rouse the children so that they wake up in good spirits, or how to guide the conversation so everyone would feel included, or how a "well heeled" doctor would look as she welcomes her patients to her office. Maybe these ideas come from those awful stereotypical sixties television sitcoms like "Ozzie and Harriet," "Donna Reed" or "Father Knows Best." Or later, watching Martha Stewart in her perfect kitchen, making the perfect meal with all the perfect pans and utensils. It's difficult not to buy into that nonsense. I know I did. Add to that my insecurities and natural perfectionism and I was beginning to understand how I became driven, thinking I could have it all without paying the price of disease. This is what I needed to heal; I wanted to accept and relax into my own life.

Our bodies tell us when things are out of balance. They try to get our attention with little signs like fever blisters or canker sores, headaches or backaches, indigestion and/or gas, yeast infections and lethargy. The challenge is to slow down and listen and not to ignore or override these symptoms because they provide a plethora of information: fever blisters signal too much stress; gas often occurs from eating too much fatty foods; yeast infections commonly arise due to too much sugar, and fermented products like wine; and indigestion can indicate excessive intake of coffee and acidic foods as well as overeating. The body gives us these milder messages first but many of us refuse to listen. At that moment, I was dying to listen.

CHAPTER ELEVEN

Earth's Whisper

Here is a story
to break your heart.
Are you willing?
This winter
the loons came to our harbor
and died, one by one,
of nothing we could see.
A friend told me
of one on the shore
that lifted its head and opened
the elegant beak and cried out
in the long, sweet savoring of its life
which, if you have heard it,
you know is a sacred thing,
and for which, if you have not heard it,
you had better hurry to where
they still sing.
And, believe me, tell no one
just where that is.
The next morning
this loon, speckled
and iridescent and with a plan
to fly home
to some hidden lake,
was dead on the shore.
I tell you this
To break your heart,
by which I mean only
that it break open and never close again
to the rest of the world.

Mary Oliver

A few months prior to my cancer diagnosis, my husband had asked me what I wanted for my fiftieth birthday. I knew exactly what I wanted: a waterscape. I wanted to hear those calming, gurgling, water sounds surrounding me. It would start on high ground, meandering around the side of the house, with three or four waterfalls, culminating in a large pond full of brightly colored koi. I wanted the brilliantly colored purple and yellow plants, whose name I don't know but that I had seen in pictures; and I wanted cottontails. My husband didn't hesitate; soon, we met with a landscape architect and he drew up plans for this wonderful addition to our home.

We broke ground six weeks before my birthday. Just writing those words, "breaking ground" breaks my heart. Ever since my twenties, I have reacted to our seemingly endless assault of the Earth. John would invite me on a date and take me to see projects he designed that were in various stages of construction. Wherever they had broken ground, I would gasp at the deep, raw earth and I could swear I heard the ground weeping. Years later, just before beginning construction of the waterscape, I spoke about my concern to my shaman friend, Maria. She advised us to create a ceremony asking our friends and neighbors. And so we did. Maria came with her husband, and we gathered our friends and neighbors together. One friend came dressed in authentic American Indian regalia, complete with a feathered headdress, soft brown deer skin clothing and beaded moccasins. We gathered in a circle and began drumming. Then Matthew, Maria's husband, began singing and chanting and we all joined in. The children were hooting and hollering, running around spreading tobacco and corn meal. Then, with great reverence, Maria offered prayers to Mother Earth asking if we could use the land to bring the joy of the rivers into our back yard, if we could take away some of her land in the spirit of offering back to her our gratitude. She said that my heart was yearning for the sound of water to be close and comfort me and she asked for the earth's blessing. Just as she concluded her prayer, we saw a magnificent blue heron flying slowly and majestically just over our heads as if to say, "Yes, you have permission." We were all speechless.

The pond was completed on my birthday, the same day I learned I had breast cancer. All summer long, as I fought for my life, the beautiful waterscape was my salvation – the koi and the blue heron – my constant companions.

In Chinese oral history, blue Heron represents regeneration. It is also believed that when a Koi dies, it represents part of a person dying. What rich metaphors for what was happening in my body and soul! I wanted all the cancer to die; I wanted to be regenerated. So when the blue heron showed up at our pond, I was ecstatic; I knew it was a sign that everything would be all right.

Koi, or nushikigoi in Japanese, literally means "brocaded carp." Originally found in China, they were coveted by the Japanese for whom they symbolized "perseverance in adversity" and "overcoming life difficulties." There are many varieties of koi. Their appearance is similar to a very large and very vibrantly colored gold fish. Many are iridescent and at night they shimmered and shined as they swam by the lights of our pond. My favorite is the iridescent blue one. Depending on the variety, koi can cost from one hundred to thousands of dollars per fish. Our Koi seemed to be healthy and happy in their new surroundings, until - the blue heron showed up. This was not a match made in heaven but a perfect match in the natural world – hunter and hunted.

The Great Blue Heron is about four feet tall with a five to six foot wingspan and a very long neck. His face is white and he has a black stripe down the back of his head. His magnificent wings are two-tone - blue and grey. We were in love with this majestic bird. When he would land at the pond, I would say, "Oh, my God, the blue heron," with great joy. But then I would turn to the koi and say, fretfully, "Oh, my God, the koi." I was secretly delighted every time I saw this gorgeous creature fly away with a koi in his mouth because I wanted to believe what the Chinese believed, that this dying Koi represented big chunks of my cancer dying off. Regeneration.

Towards summer's end, we decided, while we didn't mind feeding the Blue such extravagant meals, we did have a responsibility to protect the koi. So the dance began. Every time the blue heron appeared, we would run towards him clapping our hands to demand he leave before he filled his belly, or else . . . I don't think it did much good, but it made us feel better.

We talked to experts about our situation, which was so personal and grave to us. We were told, "It's just the way it is; birds have been eating fish since time immemorial." We knew all this. We were told to put netting over the pond which we simply couldn't do because we were afraid the heron would become entangled. So we built scarecrows, changing them every two or three days to fool the heron. We used clothing, pots and pans, tinfoil, and an oversized teddy bear sitting on an Adirondack chair with tinfoil on his head. He wasn't to be fooled though. When he left at the end of September, he was much bigger and healthier than when he arrived. Though he left us koi poor, we had been immersed in the dance all summer and it kept our minds and hearts busy.

Nature is an exquisite teacher and I was her devoted student that summer. I brought in two other doctors to help me with my practice and I spent many hours a day sitting by the waterscape. I learned that the water flows, sometimes smooth and easy, sometimes rough and agitated, just like our lives. There were obstacle like rocks, plants, algae, but the water kept flowing and circling back around. I determined that I could fight the current of life or I could enjoy the ride. It's my choice.

The heron always knew what he wanted. Sometimes he would wait for hours, patiently, until the time was right, then he would go in for the kill. If he didn't get the fish the first time, he continued until he was successful. No dramatics, he just waited. It was beautiful to observe.

The koi have a very interesting community. Whenever we introduced a new fish to the clan, the largest fish had to approve of this new member. He would swim out from the school of fish, circle the newcomer, and seemingly invite him to join the rest of the clan. In minutes, it was as though he had always been a part of the school. Observing the dance of nature was an exquisite focus for me that summer.

When my husband asked what I wanted for my fiftieth birthday, I suspect that I knew, in that deep knowing place, that I would need immense strength, courage and comfort on the journey facing me; that I would need to hear the voice of God whispering to me through the natural world; and that I would need to dance.

Following the completion of my treatment for cancer, I slowly regained my strength and stamina. I began working more and the doctors covering my practice returned to their own practices. But I had changed. I no longer fit into the demands of a busy chiropractic practice, although I persevered for a year. Then I took an eight-month sabbatical with the intention of returning to practice. However, when the eight months were over, my spirit no longer resonated with the force and physicality of manipulating bones so, after twenty-two years, I gave up my chiropractic practice but retained my acupuncture practice. That was a pivotal moment for me: I was learning to not only listen to my inner voice, but to act on it - which has always been more difficult.

Much of those eight months were spent with my mother who was in the process of dying. I felt privileged to accompany her for a while, to observe her courage and grace.

On August 4, 2004 at 7:30 a.m., I was swimming at Mount Tom Pond with my friends. Suddenly two ospreys began circling above me, then one broke away, swept down in front of me, dive bombed a fish and then they both flew away. I said to my friends, "That's Mom; she has left her body." When I got home, I called my Dad and she had indeed passed over during my swim.

My two dear friends and I have been swimming the length of Mount Tom Pond (which is actually a lake) for twenty years. The season is short in Connecticut and we relish this time from June to mid-September for its warmth and beauty. Gathering in the early morning as the sun rises over the lush rolling hills is one of my life's greatest joys. Over the years it has become much more than a swim; it is a daily celebration of our lives and the beauty that surrounds us. I never tire of the most marvelous show on earth – the rising and setting of the sun.

We have little company this early in the morning but the company we keep is unparalleled: the blue heron, cormorants, osprey, ducks and ducklings, and an occasional eagle. Over the years, we have fancied ourselves to be three beautiful sirens swimming in the heavy mist and fog of early morning as the warm air meets frigid water. We watch as the sun, that exquisite red burst of flame, peaks out over Mt. Tom and begins to shimmer across the cobalt blue lake, and we breathe it deeply into our souls.

We gave up the wet suits early on because they were too confining and, as we aged, impossible to squeeze into. Instead, we stand on the dock, tea or coffee in hand, moving, jumping and gyrating to warm our bodies until one of us says, "enough, it's time" and then we plunge into the cold water. Once we are all in, we swim as fast as our legs can flutter until we feel warmed by the energy of our moving bodies and by the strong morning sun which by this point is beaming down on our faces and shoulders.

These swims have sustained us through raising our children, raising our husbands, affairs, heartache, backache, surgeries, cancer, deaths, births, adventures, and sadness – bone-wrenching sadness. Our little piece of heaven is as much about coming together in friendship with nature as our witness, as it is about exercise. So it was appropriate that during the most sacred part of my day, my mother transitioned. I had prayed that she would die peacefully and in the end, I think she had a beautiful death; she slipped across the threshold with ease and comfort in her sleep.

When significant people in our lives die, a shift takes place in our psyche and spirit that gives us the opportunity to grow and develop in a powerful way. I have seen women blossom and become stronger following the death of a dominant male figure. I have seen men soften and choose more compatible partners when their wives die. And most often, I have seen older children change direction when they no longer have a parent who they are trying to please.

When my mother passed, I felt the shift of "mother energy" from the mother who had birthed me to our Earth Mother.   The earth, in all her splendor, was enticing me to come closer, to become her apprentice, and to grow through her tutelage. I was both tentative and excited to become her student.

My first brave adventure was in February of 2005, when I participated in a vision quest in Death Valley. I knew very little about this Native American tradition; I only knew that I loved Chief Joseph of the Nez Perez. That was the sum total of my pull towards a vision quest. And yet I committed to eleven days out in the wilderness, four of which I was completely alone, fasting, frightened to death and hopeful that I would receive clarity, direction, purpose or simply a greater understanding of life. It was truly a magical, sacred experience and I took away from that experience a palpable reverence for the sacred and divine in nature and a greater understanding of the oneness of the human and other than human world. I carry this with me always.

I continued to feel a need to know nature in her rawest, most natural presentation. Tibet was calling to me. She had been calling me for ten years, ever since I read Robert Thurman's book, *Circling the Sacred Mountain*. In May of 2006, I answered the call and I took a five-week pilgrimage to circumambulate the Sacred Mountain, Mt. Kailash, in western Tibet. For the faith traditions of the Hindu, Buddhist, Jain and Bon, this is considered the most sacred pilgrimage. Although I embrace the Buddhist philosophy and lifestyle, I am not a committed member of any of those traditions. So it was a mystery to me why I felt pulled to do this trip. Nonetheless, I listened to my inner wisdom and prepared for the trip.

It was a challenging trip for me in so many ways, not the least of which was trying desperately to breathe at those higher elevations of 13,000 – 19,000 feet. That thin air is no place for asthmatics. I was also surprised at the primitive conditions in the country. Perhaps I simply hadn't thought it through, but I was ill prepared for the lack of indoor plumbing, or any plumbing for that matter. Yet, experiencing Tibet and her people was a dramatic and powerful experience for me – my heart was changed irrevocably for having been there.

I was successful at completing my kora around the circumference of Mt. Kailash (the Bon religion is the only faith that travels counterclockwise around Mt. Kailash; all others travel clockwise/sunwise). I learned that about 75 percent of the pilgrims doing the kora during the Saga Dawa festival in 2006 had to turn back because of the altitude, weather and/or difficult terrain. I know that on the second morning of my kora, when I pulled back the flap of my tent to accept my steaming hot cup of tea from the Sherpa, I was surprised and slightly deflated to see that snow completely covered the mountain. But this day would be the longest and most difficult trek – 9 ½ hours – so it was important to stay positive. I prayed for grace and breath, had a hot breakfast and began my ascent.

The intention that you hold as you circle this Sacred Mountain is "other" directed and it is said that whatever you ask for during this pilgrimage will be granted. For example, I asked for safety, love and shelter for all the children of the world, healing for our confused and angry youth, and peace for Tibet. You are not meant to ask for personal gain. Following the circumambulation, to wash away all your sins (this part sounds strangely Catholic), you bathe in the mountain lake of Mansarovar. Because the lake is shallow for quite some distance and because the sun is incredibly fierce at that elevation, it was not at all cold. That surprised me because the elevation was 18,000 plus. Here, at the lake, and throughout Tibet, I often felt a sacred, calming presence.

This pilgrimage was for me a deeply spiritual and life-changing experience but I cannot tell you exactly how or why. Perhaps it was walking side by side other pilgrims of other faiths all with the common purpose of devotion; perhaps it was those gorgeous yaks and all the yak butter tea I drank to keep warm and healthy; maybe it was the countless monasteries we walked through on the way to Mt. Kailash and on the way back to Nepal – all of which had changed dramatically since the Dalai Lama was forced out of his country; perhaps it was the sweet energy of Mt. Kailash herself or the energy of the hundreds of thousands of pilgrims who had gone before me for the single purpose of devotion. Or maybe it was those three stones I picked up from the ground and heard, with each separate one, "Be still, Be at ease, Be with God." It's not that I can't articulate what happened to me up there in that unearthly altitude; it is that I simply don't know. I don't know why my soul needed to make this pilgrimage to feel complete but I am able to embrace the mystery with immeasurable gratitude. I am also so very thankful to Bharat, my kind and generous Sherpa who followed me all the way up the mountain like a precious, blessed shadow. He continuously repeated this mantra, "Veeery slowly, Mom. Slow like a caterpillar. One foot and then the other. Look up now, see God, meditate. That's right Mom. Veeery slowly now." And he kept this up for three days. I was the oldest of the five of us on this pilgrimage and he called me Mom out of respect. The average life expectancy for Nepalese men is 49, and for Tibetan men is 47 and I was over 50 so that is ancient by those standards. Bharat also showed me the most sacred places along the kora that were hidden from the public and the ritual involved with each place. I learned so much from him, and from so many of the Nepalese and Tibetans, about true devotion; it is something I had never experienced before and it was deeply moving. Everything they see is an opportunity to honor God with a bow or a kora (circling around it) or both. Even bowing and saying, "Namaste" which they do in Nepal, is honoring the God within each of us. I also learned about One Breath. I called upon that breath to accompany me on that journey, at 19,000 feet, around Mt. Kailash. I needed the breath of the world to keep my lungs inflated. I have always felt that the world shares one heart and one soul but I never thought much about breath until I didn't have any.

I am honored to have had this magical experience, whatever the reason.

I realize my trip to Tibet was my last attempt at trying to fill myself up; to become a better me so that I would never again have cancer as an opportunity to grow. I have not looked outward for completion since that trip. In fact, I have taken very few trips since then. I missed my family and my home terribly: I ached for my husband and I realized that he is home to me; I realized how blessed we are in this country with our freedom and our comforts; I realize that this incarnation for me has been a rich, sacred gift; I know that happiness has always been right here and that it was a choice to allow sadness, loneliness and disconnection to be a part of me; It is also a choice to let it go. It has taken awhile for this to sink in.

My propensity to run in circles shifted during my kora in the heavenly altitudes in Tibet. I believe I circled back to myself and I feel more at home now. None of that turning and circling had anything to do with a wrong turn. It was a turn inward and it was right for me.

Moving to Connecticut and to the country brought me closer to the sacred; she was everywhere. Her presence was quiet and soft and not at all demanding: the rolling hills, the exquisite sunrises and sunsets, the deer grazing contently beneath my bedroom window in the morning, the occasional bobcat, fox and mountain lion; the melting snow and warmth in spring calling to the winged ones to begin nesting, and the heat of summer giving way to the autumn chill as the trees burst into a burning flame of color. And through all this, I was an observer – I held back from getting my hands dirty. But that was soon to change.

CHAPTER TWELVE

A Kind of Dying

Tell a wise person, or else keep silent,
because the massman will mock it right away.
I praise what is truly alive,
What longs to be burned to death.

In the calm of the water of the love-nights,
where you were begotten, where you have begotten,
a strange feeling comes over you.
When you can see the silent candle burning.

Now you are no longer caught
in obsession with darkness,
and a desire for higher lovemaking
sweeps you upward.

Distance does not make you falter,
Now arriving in magic, flying,
and, finally, insane for the light,
you are the butterfly and you are gone.

And so long as you haven't experienced
this; to die and so to grow,
you are only a troubled guest
on the dark earth.

The Holy Longing

JW von Goethe
(trans Robert Bly)

There have been many opportunities in my life to grow; many of them I wouldn't have chosen - but I had to be stopped, dead in my tracks, to understand the message deep in my soul. I can express many things intellectually and sometimes they are heartfelt, but to put my awareness into practice, and to live what I know, to embody my knowing, is a constant struggle. Forced to slow down, truly listen, and then live the lesson, has changed me irrevocably. It is these pivotal moments, often wrapped in the most awful packages that have given me the greatest opportunities for grace, gratitude and transformation.

On the day of my five-year checkup with my oncologist, the day cancer patients look forward to as a rite of passage; I was told I had metastatic breast cancer. I now had two grapefruit-sized tumors, one on each ovary. While I would tell you that I was completely blind-sided by this news that would not be true. I suspected something because I requested the necessary diagnostic tests, just as I had the first time I was diagnosed. I did not take my second cancer diagnosis graciously. I did not want to hear it, talk about it, or do anything about it. I was heartbroken and believed my body had betrayed me. I had the surgery quickly and then withdrew. I didn't want to talk to my oncologist because I knew I would not do chemotherapy again. I didn't want to talk to my friends because I didn't want to discuss treatment options and I did not want to incur their disapproval. I was angry at God that once was not enough and I was angry at myself because I hadn't done a better job of healing. And, I was angry at God and myself for not having been clear with one another about what was expected of me in the world; I felt I wasn't living my life correctly. I believed I wouldn't have been given this message repeatedly if I had "gotten" it the first time. I began considering the possibility that it was time to die. I was tired, bone tired. I hadn't learned to live differently and the way I was living was killing me. And I no longer had the energy or the inclination to continue working on myself; I was done digging into my psyche trying to pull out a better me. I no longer had children at home so I felt less guilty about dying and leaving them motherless. I reflected on my many accomplishments and I concluded that I had managed to create a rich, fulfilling life: I had lived all over the world; I went to undergraduate, graduate and medical school; I married and raised two beautiful children; I had worked as a physician successfully for twenty-five years and as a seeker, I explored many of the wonders of the physical and spiritual world. The more I thought about it, the more comfortable I felt with the idea of death and the end of my struggle. Freedom. Ease. I wanted freedom and ease.

I told my husband I might be ready to die and asked how he would feel about it. In his very dear, New England way, he said, "That won't work for me at all; in no way would that work for me." I understood that this was his way of telling me that he loved me and wanted me around for a long, long time.

As the weeks passed, the idea of dying began to frighten me and yet it still had a certain appeal. I was tired of trying so hard to be more successful, a better wife, a better mom, a better doctor, to be closer to the Divine, stronger mentally, emotionally and spiritually and it was the end of that struggle that sounded so sweet to me. Interestingly, no one had said that I was going to die and I felt the surgery had been successful in removing all the cancer. Nevertheless, I felt suspended between two worlds.

My friends were frightened and distraught because I was not my usual cheerleader self. They began calling twice a day, in the morning and evening. They said they had convened a pow-wow and out of concern for me, were checking in. I was moved by their love and attention but I was still withdrawn.

The holidays were coming and I waded through Thanksgiving. When Christmas arrived, we flew to California to be with our son and daughter. We would not have a Christmas tree this year which made sense, I told myself, because why cut down a precious tree if I'm not around to enjoy it.

I told my oncologist I would come in for a discussion after the holidays. I cancelled that appointment. I made a second and a third appointment and cancelled them too. I agreed to try a treatment but I became terribly sick and knew that I could not get well if I got that sick first. While it wasn't his first choice for me, Jedd gave me the option of "watchful waiting," meaning that I would undergo no further treatments, but I would undergo more testing more often to verify that the cancer had not come back. I agreed to go through a battery of tests every six months.

It became my sole responsibility to get well. I started juicing, went back to a vegetarian diet, did colonics regularly, stopped exercising obsessively and saw a homeopathic physician. What he said to me changed everything. After a lengthy consultation, he chose a remedy and told me to do two things: prepare to die, and start having fun. Both seemed impossible. Then he said, "And for God's sake, drop out of the seminary, you aren't having any fun and they have nothing to teach you." Back when I had stopped practicing, I enrolled in the seminary because it was something I always wanted to do. But he was right, I wasn't having fun and I wasn't learning what I had hoped I would.

I asked what he meant by preparing to die and he said I would have to figure this out. He said the same thing when I asked how I would learn to have fun at fifty-six. He prescribed the homeopathic remedy called conium, also known as hemlock, which symbolizes death.

For the next two weeks, I obsessed over what this doctor was advising me to do. Did he mean to prepare to die literally, or symbolically? Was he clairvoyant and able to see that my body was dying? I decided he meant to prepare myself for death metaphorically and so I researched and performed many ceremonies, including the Native American death lodge and The Tibetan Book of Living and Dying ceremony of death. During this process, I decided I wanted to live. Not merely exist – I wanted to be fully alive. I had to face death head on to appreciate my life; I had to die to be reborn. It was a particularly auspicious time because it was Easter 2008. Easter always falls on the first Sunday following the first full moon which follows the first day of spring. I find the symbolism of Easter, the Death and Resurrection of Jesus, exquisite. I love this concept of letting the old go and embracing the new; rising above the suffering and pain and embracing renewal. And it comes at the most auspicious time; spring, with all its new growth and new beginnings. This particular Easter, the idea of rebirth and coming back to life was particularly resonant with me.

I had told the homeopath that I was tired of the sadness and suffering in my life and in the world and that my one true longing was for unity with God. So, along with symbolically preparing to die, I also read book after book on awakening, enlightenment, realization and coming alive. Ironically, I had read similar books thirty-five years earlier. At that point, my spiritual seeking led me to a guru from whom I received shaktipat, or awakening of the kundulini energy. We all have latent kundalini or spiritual energy that lies at the base of the spine and people on a spiritual journey often feel that this awakening is necessary for spiritual advancement. While my earlier efforts toward unity were more sporadic and naïve, I now wondered if I had grown spiritually at all over the last thirty-five years and that question was painfully deflating.

After eight months, I slowly felt myself emerging from the darkness. I began to feel a shift, both in my spiritual practice and in my everyday life. I hadn't felt sadness or suffering for months, I was still withdrawn but I felt content. The most surprising and transformative moment came when I realized I no longer wanted to practice as an acupuncturist. So, I closed my practice. I didn't know how I would justify my existence - what I would say when people asked what I was doing now that I wasn't practicing. In essence, I wasn't who I had been: I was no longer a daughter as my mother had passed away, or a mother to my children who were on their own; I was no longer employed as a doctor and a healer. And I no longer had cancer. This shift was at once terrifying and completely freeing. I vacillated between each and was flabbergasted by the euphoria I felt with the death of the persona: Dr. Martin. It was a sweet relief to no longer hold myself to such a high standard and to feel I had to help people who other practitioners had been unable to help. I was completely unaware that I felt that way; I thought I loved my work, but in letting it go, I felt I was coming back to life. Although I remained uncertain and cautious, I felt myself rising up slowly; something was changing. Maybe these dying little deaths were a good thing, like the ebb and flow of the ocean and the rising and falling of the moon and the sun. We are constantly dying and re-birthing, but it is perhaps so subtle that we hardly notice. I felt I was breaking the chains that bound me, easing into myself the way I would lower myself into a bath when it is too hot: slow, tentative, slipping in then coming out, until I am completely immersed. I was finally willing to relinquish all the identities that had bound me to my own expectations of performance and perfection. I created this bondage myself; I bound myself out of fear - fear of failure, fear of not being good enough, fear of mediocrity and invisibility and fear of boredom. I believed that to be bored or boring was tantamount to being nobody at all. As I write this, I realize I have become beautifully boring. I eased into it with grace and dignity and I find comfort in my slower, less demanding life.

As I emerged from that dark night of the soul, I experienced a strong impulse to put my hands in the dirt. I was never a gardener; in fact, I am notorious for killing anything that grows. Yet, my heart was longing to plant something in the earth. I began with a vegetable garden and then a flower garden. In my discovery of the joys of gardening, I finally understood, first hand, what my friends, family, and patients had been talking about all these years. It is joyful, and it is worth all the subsequent aches and pains. But my greatest joy came one sunny day in May, 2008. I was gazing out the kitchen window toward the southwest and I saw the most magnificent boulder sitting out in the field, all by itself, vibrating a sound. I had never seen this huge boulder before. I was convinced it was a miracle, that this boulder was dropped from the heavens. When my husband John came in from working the fields, I asked him about it. He said he was finally sick to death of hitting this boulder with his tractor every time he mowed the field so he upended it and left it there. I was so glad! It was shimmery white, about four feet wide and five feet tall, one side was perfectly flat and it rounded out on the other side and I suddenly knew I would build a medicine wheel with that stone as the center stone.

I am blessed to have a supportive husband who goes along with most of my zany ideas. I designed the wheel and used as much stone from our land as we could and then ordered another couple of tons from a quarry. I knew that building a medicine wheel would involve intense physical labor and muscle and I was up for the challenge. However, I didn't anticipate what happened. The week after we began the project, my horse spooked and I flew into the air, and landed on my right wrist which I broke in three places. This made hauling stones incredibly difficult and painful. So, with enthusiasm and great fascination with the entire concept of a medicine wheel, John began working with me side by side doing all the heavy work by hand and with the tractor. My husband has a deep love affair with stone: he picks one up, holds it in his hands, feeling the different surfaces – smooth, rough, and sharp, then he begins to look at it from all angles - in sunlight and out; he becomes one with the stone, and his eyes glaze over like an adolescent hopelessly in love. Each stone seems to have a life of its own. Finally, he carefully places it where he feels the stone wishes to be. It's like a sacred dance. So the two of us worked on the wheel together for many weeks and when it was close to being complete, we invited our dear friends and neighbors to the north, east and south to bring a stone to represent their direction and join us in ceremony. As we gathered for the ritual, we asked Mother/Father Creator to bless our medicine wheel, to bring harmony to the land and her people and to spread this harmony outward.

While there are different ways to construct a medicine wheel, the basic concept comes from Native American Indian astrology and solar cycles. The design can be complex or simple: we kept it simple. The center stone called the Creator stone represents the Divine. We have placed the seven smaller stones, representing the four directions, plus above (heaven), below (earth), and inside (spirit), three feet out from the creator stone. Seven feet out from there, we placed the larger four directions stones representing north, east, south, and west. In between each of these stones are three smaller stones which represent the moons in each season, like the months of the year. There is also rich symbolism in the materials we used to build the medicine wheel. For example, Belgium blocks were placed around the circumference of the wheel. They are made of granite and its energy helps us to see the big picture and defeats negativity; it helps in maintaining balance in relationships and provides stability and grounding. The path just inside the circumference is paved with white marble chips which represent serenity and aids in meditative or controlled thoughts. When we walk the medicine wheel, we walk sunwise. The circle has no beginning and no end; it represents movement and change. We move from the South, the summer of our lives which is a time of innocence to the West, the direction of the setting sun and uncertainty, our shadow side, onward to the North, the winter of our lives, a time of wisdom and love of others, finally reaching the East which is in the realm of spirit and regeneration. We circle around and around during our lifetime from vision and inspiration (east), through childlike laughter and ease (south), to deep emotional truth (west) and reach wisdom and elder hood (north); birth, death and rebirth. This symbolism is very dear to me.

And so each morning as the sun comes up, I grab a cup of tea and my dog, Dudley and head down to the medicine wheel to offer a prayer of gratitude and hope for this life I am living, for Mother Earth and for all of us who inhabit her, human and other than human. Then, I listen with an open heart.

CONCLUSION

Tormented friend, why do you still enquire
And thirst to know the sum of things entire?
The more you strive, the less you will succeed:
Striving too hard begets a troubled mind
And those who strive will always stay confined
But LIGHT IMMORTAL, mortally enshrined

So live in bliss – enjoy the simple task;
Seek not to know, and do not dare to ask
Why you are here or what your fate will be.
Be still and listen to the symphony
Which your surroundings play in unity.
The part cannot exist without the whole;
The whole cannot exist without the part;
And reason has no place in cosmic art.

When stillness reigns, you are the sum of things;
The Nothing and the All that Oneness brings.
When stillness reigns, you are Infinity
And sense the nearness of Divinity.
Just as the pigeon navigates in flight
And homeward speeds before a hint of night;
So too, the soul, will homeward soar one day
Without a mind to guide it on its way.

STILLNESS
By Robert Goslin

These days I am a gardener and a writer. Though alien to me a few short years ago, now when I describe myself this way a sweet smile creeps into my heart and across my face and I feel giddy with love. I suppose we have many lives and possibilities living inside us if only we can circumvent the bone-chilling fear that stands in our way of claiming our life. This takes practice and patience and with time, it becomes easier.

When I look back on my two encounters with cancer, I have to smile at how differently I reacted: The first time I wanted to become more, learn more, find the missing piece, add to myself so that I would have what I needed to combat the illness. The second time I knew I had to be less, to empty out all that I was to get back to my true essence. Each response was appropriate at the time.

The Scottish poet, Norman Caig's, poem, "The Present" begins like this:

I give you emptiness,
I give you plentitude,
unwrap them carefully,"

John O'Donohue, the Irish poet and philosopher, says that this poem
"suggests the dual rhythm of emptiness and plentitude at the heart of the life of the soul. Nothingness is the sister of possibility. It makes an urgent space for that which is new, surprising, and unexpected. When you feel nothingness and emptiness gnawing at your life, there is no need for despair. This is a call from your soul, awakening your life to new possibilities."

Life is full of detours, roundabouts, U-turns, eight-lane freeways, back roads, and dead ends. Regardless of the path, you will ultimately get where you are going. I am a backroads kind of gal; I get where I am going on the less traveled roads. Robert Frost spoke beautifully about this in his poem, The Road Less Traveled:

. . . I took the one less traveled by,
And that has made all the difference

All my life, I have felt like an odd duck, but I have always been able to find my flock; they accept and love me, idiosyncrasies and all. And if I have learned anything from my experiences, it's this: the key is love and acceptance. One of my most difficult tasks has been to love and accept myself. I don't know why this is such a challenge. I can repeat what I've been told by countless psychotherapists and other therapists and it is probably true. I know that until I totally love and accept myself, I can't truly love and accept others unconditionally. Lack of love is a big problem in relationships. And it seems that the most important thing that humans have is our relationships. I know that when I am feeling small, I look for a scapegoat for my misery and it is usually the ones I love the most, my husband and my children.

I used to believe that I was my greatest fan because I truly enjoyed my own company. I know now that this was more about the ease of not having to interact with others than actually loving my own company. I mistook my natural introverted tendency of liking to be alone for loving myself. There is a huge difference between the two. I have begun the process of moving away from loving and acknowledging myself for my accomplishments to simply loving who I am. It has been a learning process that started with focused intent and small exercises and, over time, it has become easier. I think that opening to ourselves is our most natural way of being and yet, with life's hurts and challenges, it becomes difficult and murky. I know I started life as pure perfection and love but I strayed so far away that it has almost killed me coming home.

I now have a greater understanding of how all the convoluted happenings in my life wiped out my confidence and left self-loathing. So, I am becoming a newer, reconditioned model of myself, replacing self-hatred with love. This understanding, however hard won, has lead me to the realization that there are no wrong turns in life. I wanted to believe that, if I could find where I had diverged onto a path that had lead to illness, I could backtrack to that point, make the correction, and life would be back on track. I needed to believe it would be that simple in order to not freak out. But, life isn't cut and dry; it isn't black or white or right or wrong. Illness is not a punishment for bad behavior or poor choices. I made the right choices at the time that I made them. Later, when the choices came back around, with more understanding and more love in my heart, I made different choices. I didn't have cancer because I had bad genes or because I abused my body. And, cancer had nothing to do with a wrong turn. I now believe in my purest heart, that I agreed to accept cancer as a learning opportunity in this lifetime and that the time had come to receive the lesson and learn from it, which is what I have done. There is no blame for how I turned out or didn't turn out. It isn't like that. I agreed to come into this life and grow and become and I have done that in the best way that I know. If life was sometimes more difficult than I would have liked, it is not because I was abused or raped, was taught by nuns who terrified me, moved around from country to country every couple of years, had a brother who was schizophrenic or a mother who loved me too much. It wasn't because my husband is not warm and fuzzy or that my kids often think I am a bit overbearing or that I sometimes feel that I am a square peg in a round hole. It is not because I gave at the office, literally, with all my heart and soul until I was bone dry; nor is it because I was a "Suzy saccharin social worker" or because I had cancer. It is not because I am not yet a realized being or because God doesn't love me enough. It is not because I am a seeker who hasn't found what she's seeking. It is just because it is my journey. That's all. There is no one or no thing at fault; no blame. But there is deep, reverent gratitude for the gift of all of these opportunities. Without them, I may not have broken wide open with a wild thrust into the world. I may not have made choices that could have killed me but that brought me back to myself; like circling the Sacred Mountain at 19,000 feet with asthma, or facing my fears and crying for a vision alone in the cold, dark, rainy desert (It was the first time in one hundred years the desert had been so saturated with rain that it bloomed); or traveling for two years to see my heart's desires in Europe. I could have missed all these and many more opportunities, like cancer, but I chose to act on them. And that has made all the difference.

My life was spent searching far and wide, only to ultimately come home to myself. It is like traveling in the car to get to my friend's home in another state, only to return home again the next day. There is so much that flashes by my car windows: cows, barns, horses, stadiums, chemical plants, lakes, mountains and then, ultimately, I am there. I had to pass all those things to get where I was going. Some of those images pass by without much notice, like stadiums and chemical plants or even proms and class reunions; and others, like the mountains and lakes, or perhaps rape and cancer, they really pulled me in. However, they weren't really germane to my ultimate destination, I just thought they were. It is my mind that makes a big deal out of things; it won't let anything go. But once an event has occurred, it's over, gone, past, no longer significant. And it does feel good to be home.

I often think of Jesus' journey to Mt. Calvary: To prepare for His death, He had already fasted for 40 days and 40 nights (I am cranky after three days). Then He began the painful, heartbreaking climb to Mt. Calvary, carrying a brutally heavy cross, the mixture of blood and sweat dripping down His face from the crown of thorns He wore on His head. He suffered deep, heartbreaking pain and humiliation as He traveled along His path. He knew this was a necessary part of the journey and He also knew that He would be resurrected; that was His Destiny. The journey was simply the journey but coming home was what mattered.

So heart-wrenching was the pain that I felt at different crossroads on my journey that I feared I would not get passed it; I feared I would die. Then I would dig a little deeper, grab hold of unencumbered, disentangled love and forgiveness and hold it close until I became that. Then I could move on, because just like the buildings and events that flash past the window on our journey – they were gone, in the past, and no longer significant. This is how I often feel these days, but not always. Sometimes I still want to hold onto anger and blame, so I do, until it passes by the window of my heart.

Life has humbled me, made me more human and expanded me all at once. I am so grateful that the natural state of my soul, underpinning each moment of my life, burns with determination for deep investigation into those dark, hidden places I was petrified to approach. I did not want to go there. I wanted to believe in purity, goodness and light; not pain and sorrow. I didn't want to acknowledge the existence of darkness for fear it would envelope me and pull me into its abyss. But once uncovered and embraced, I was given the light, breath and wings to soar. It is this that has made my life rich and magical. It is also my inquisitive spirit that has driven me to seek and find that which resonates with who I am in relationship to all that is. Suffering is often a choice I made, and yet that misery eventually took me to the antithesis of that – to joy. I made choices in life that ultimately took me home to myself but I would have told you at the time, kicking and screaming, that those incidents were not my choice. Our life is our choice.

These days, the challenges along my journey seem easier; and I'm not taking myself so seriously. I have finally taken my children's advice and "lightened up." That pleases me. That pleases me very much and easier is good. It tells me that I no longer believe that if I am not suffering, I am not doing life correctly. These subtle adjustments to who I am, are a breath of fresh air: brighter and more spacious. That's progress and that's good enough for me.

ACKNOWLEDGEMENTS

My heartfelt thanks go to my deceased mother, Dorothy, and my father, John, for bringing me into this world. I also thank my four siblings: Carolyn, Dick, Judy and Danny. These are the people who have loved me and helped shape who I am. Special thanks go to my older brother, Dick, who passed away during the final stages of this book. He was a profound presence in my life and provided me with many stories. And I thank my husband, John, for his continued support and encouragement throughout the process of birthing and writing this book. He is my greatest fan! Great thanks also go to my friends – Judy Einbinder and Chez Liley, and my friend and sister-in-law, Carol Martin - for their editing, hand holding and support. Finally, I thank my dear friend, Diane Rossman, who took valuable time out of her busy life to edit my manuscript. She said it was a labor of love. For me, her contribution was a beautiful, transforming gift.